Refactoring Legacy T-SQL for Improved Performance

Modern Practices for
SQL Server Applications

Lisa Bohm

Apress®

Refactoring Legacy T-SQL for Improved Performance: Modern Practices for SQL Server Applications

Lisa Bohm
Chardon, OH, USA

ISBN-13 (pbk): 978-1-4842-5580-3
https://doi.org/10.1007/978-1-4842-5581-0

ISBN-13 (electronic): 978-1-4842-5581-0

Managing Director, Apress Media LLC: Welmoed Spahr
Acquisitions Editor: Jonathan Gennick
Development Editor: Laura Berendson
Coordinating Editor: Jill Balzano

Cover image designed by Freepik (www.freepik.com)

Distributed to the book trade worldwide by Springer Science+Business Media New York, 233 Spring Street, 6th Floor, New York, NY 10013. Phone 1-800-SPRINGER, fax (201) 348-4505, e-mail orders-ny@springer-sbm.com, or visit www.springeronline.com. Apress Media, LLC is a California LLC and the sole member (owner) is Springer Science + Business Media Finance Inc (SSBM Finance Inc). SSBM Finance Inc is a **Delaware** corporation.

For information on translations, please e-mail rights@apress.com, or visit http://www.apress.com/rights-permissions.

Apress titles may be purchased in bulk for academic, corporate, or promotional use. eBook versions and licenses are also available for most titles. For more information, reference our Print and eBook Bulk Sales web page at http://www.apress.com/bulk-sales.

Any source code or other supplementary material referenced by the author in this book is available to readers on GitHub via the book's product page, located at www.apress.com/9781484255803. For more detailed information, please visit http://www.apress.com/source-code.

Printed on acid-free paper

This book is dedicated to Allen White, who has been my friend as well as helped me grow into a valued member of the community, and taught me how important it is to keep giving back and helping others.

Table of Contents

About the Author

Lisa Bohm leads a team of database administrators (DBAs) for a software development company. Her history with legacy database code began early in her career with a summer project to rewrite the chemical inventory database for the research division of a local VA hospital. From there, she went on to building front-end web applications. When the web calls timed out, Lisa dug in to learn what databases can do. She has since transitioned into database administration, inheriting and improving legacy applications along the way. Her personal focus remains on solid database architecture and writing well-performing T-SQL.

About the Technical Reviewer

Kathi Kellenberger is a data platform MVP and the editor of *Simple Talk* at Redgate Software. She has worked with SQL Server for over 20 years. She is also coleader of the PASS Women in Technology Virtual Group and an instructor at LaunchCode. In her spare time, Kathi enjoys spending time with family and friends, singing, and cycling.

Acknowledgments

I would like to thank all of the people who believed in me, encouraged, and pushed me to continue to grow and learn. Special thanks go to Mindy Curnutt, Eric Blinn, and Tim Tarbet, who showed me how amazing someone can be at the job they choose to do, and believed that I could be that good too.

I cannot leave out the people who work for me. I lead a wonderful team of involved people who are active in their continued learning, and continue to inspire me every day by finding solutions to really difficult problems.

Also thank you to my family (including my #sqlfamily) who have always been supportive, loving, and unstinting of hugs and moral support when needed!

Introduction

What is legacy code? There are a few definitions floating around out there, but as a working definition, we're going to use the following:

Legacy code is code that is no longer being actively supported by the people who wrote it.

Why are we going to use that? In software development, good documentation goes a long way. Developers should understand what code is trying to accomplish and how it's trying to do so. When documentation either doesn't exist or isn't as thorough as required and the original programmers aren't available if you need to know why something was written a particular way, it can be a nightmare to fix. In some cases, it may not even be clear whether code ever worked as intended, or if the functionality of the change someone is requesting is within the original intent of the programmer(s).

A Tale of Woe

How does legacy code start? Let's look at this story. Code is written to solve a problem – for example, someone is copying data into Excel every day and doing some hand manipulation to generate a graph to add to a larger report. A developer sets up a quick application to pull the data from the database and export it into Excel automatically for the user, also performing the calculations the user was doing by hand.

This user then trains their successor and another person in the department on how to view this report. One of them says, "Hey, this is great! Can you also make it pull data for this other report and we can show how these numbers reflect against each other?" Someone else loves the additional functionality but needs the code to work in a different way, or do different statistical calculations, or needs to add an additional field on the report. That person's manager is intrigued by the functionality and wants a weekly summary report to review. Code structure starts to resemble something that is cobbled together, as multiple developers add bits of functionality over time. Oftentimes, there is little to no documentation on the functionality or the choice of code – everyone just adds a bunch of lines at the end of the code to handle the small part they were asked to develop.

Many times, front-end developers don't specialize in T-SQL, so do not usually have a deep understanding of the SQL Server optimizer. Especially in the case of "let's just add lines of code to the bottom of this to handle additional functionality," calls to the database can increase exponentially; in many cases, calls grab the same data over and over. And, oh, by now, over half the company is using this app in one way or another – or perhaps three ways. The vast majority of these uses, by the way, were never intended by anyone who had ever touched the code.

Users complain about slowness and performance. Even more frustrating, all of the other business-critical applications that use the same database(s) become slower and slower as they fight for resources and locks with the application and its chatty data calls. Also, of course, every developer that has ever touched this application has moved on or has been promoted and hasn't looked at code for years, so has no recollection of ever manipulating any code even remotely similar to this patched-together behemoth that is rampaging through the company infrastructure.

Congratulations!

You have inherited one of these types of applications, or you probably wouldn't be here reading this book. Although there will be (possibly many) times that you may want to cry, yell, or swear, this will also give you some unparalleled opportunities to be a hero and pull off some very spectacular-seeming fixes. Just remember, though, that when you really fix something amazing, most people will be completely oblivious to that fact. Then, when you do something you think is so obvious that a worm out there on the sidewalk could probably manage it, you may get so many congratulations and thanks that you'll wonder if you really did something magical. That is probably more of a general life/job observation and not related specifically to legacy code, but it's also prevalent here.

What This Book Is

This book is meant to help you, the reader, step in and identify potential issues in a specific database object relatively quickly. There are a few assumptions that go with this:

1. Hardware/hardware configuration/VM configuration has been ruled out as the performance problem.

2. External sources have been ruled out as the problem (although we all know it's really the network…).

3. The database objects that are causing concern have been identified.

We are going to continue on from the point of "Okay, this has been identified as an issue. Now what do I do with it?" Most of what we'll be doing is actually looking at the code with the help of a few performance measures and learning about best practices to help identify problem areas. You should be familiar with basic T-SQL coding syntax and techniques and how to do a bit more advanced querying.

We will cover most of the issues commonly seen by object type, as well as a couple of less common problems just for fun. Once these problem areas within the object are identified, you can then mitigate the performance issues with relatively low effort and cost. Some objects may require a much deeper dive. Once we've done some triage to help alleviate the immediate pain an object is causing, we will cover what is involved in effectively performing the deeper dive.

We also will talk about how to quickly tell if you're on the right track in terms of the fixes you want to apply. We'll go over some simple (and free) tools that can be used to measure performance, so you can document the before/after metrics to go along with the rest of the documentation you're going to be sure to add so the next poor sod (I mean the next person) who has to maintain this system will have an easier time of it!

What This Book Is Not

Magic. This book is not magic, although at times it might seem like it helps you perform some. Seriously though, there are times when things are so bad that you cannot fix them. This is pretty rare, and either myself or one of the members of my various teams has almost always managed to "just fix it," but just be aware that it is possible that something is unsalvageable. Even better, your boss should also be aware of this and have your back should you run into that situation. If you are not that fortunate, you may want to consider finding another job, but that is probably outside the scope of this book.

This is not a deep dive into indexes, statistics, or database maintenance. I'd hope that you have all of those things set up. If you do not, please go find a book that discusses those items and make sure you are doing them! If you are not in charge of the database administration specifically, talk to whoever is and make sure THEY have those bases covered. We will definitely mention indexes and statistics, but there is much more complete information on them in other places, so discussion will be more of a flyby than exhaustive information.

This is also not a way to identify problematic hardware, external forces, or database objects. We mentioned in the preceding text what the assumptions are. If you skipped those, please go back and at least read those points so we're all on the same page when we start our triage.

The Tools

We will be using a data dump from Stack Overflow. Brent Ozar kindly provided it on his web site at `www.brentozar.com/archive/2015/10/how-to-download-the-stack-overflow-database-via-bittorrent/` which he in turn got from the awesome Stack Overflow folks.

I will also include a backup with the files for the book so everyone can start on the same foot. If you want to follow along with the examples, please make sure to run the database setup script (included in the files for the book) after restoring the database backup to add the additional objects we'll be using throughout the book.

SQL Server Management Studio (SSMS) will be the code-running application of choice. It is a free download from Microsoft: `https://docs.microsoft.com/en-us/sql/ssms/download-sql-server-management-studio-ssms`

SentryOne Plan Explorer is also a free download. We will be using it to look at execution plans and performance metrics related to the plan:

`www.sentryone.com/plan-explorer`

The last tool is a web site. You can paste in your exhaustively long statistics IO/time output, and it will parse it into nice handy tables. It is worth its weight in... um... bitcoin? If you've ever spent time trying to wade through output from a cursor or loop, you'll completely understand. Please be forewarned though that there is a limit to how much you can dump in and have it still actually regurgitate output:

`http://statisticsparser.com/`

The Inconsequential (Mostly) Details

I ran examples using SSMS 18 on a Dell Latitude E7470 laptop. I set up a VM using Oracle VirtualBox. The VM had a single vCPU and 8 GB RAM. I was using SQL Server 2016 SP2 running on Server 2016 Core.

Let's Go!

Now that we've gotten that out of the way, let's pull up the code for our first painful object and go do some first aid!

PART I

Everything Is Slow

CHAPTER 1

T-SQL Triage

The most dreaded call a DBA can get is this: "Everything in the application is slow! FIX IT!"
In many cases, the database is one of the culprits of the poor performance of the legacy
code. When you are approached to deal with some of these issues, what do you do? Well,
first you identify painful code. We're going to assume that you (or someone else) have
already identified the concerning areas. Once that happens, we need to assess the situation
by answering these questions:

1. Determine how critical the situation is:

   a. Are users down?

   b. Are all users down?

   c. Is this causing the business to lose money?

2. Determine the relative effort involved:

   a. How many lines of code are involved?

   b. How many areas of the application call this code?

   c. How much of the code needs to be changed?

3. Identify problem areas in the code:

   a. What areas are causing pain?

4. Perform triage if possible.

© Lisa Bohm 2020
L. Bohm, *Refactoring Legacy T-SQL for Improved Performance*, https://doi.org/10.1007/978-1-4842-5581-0_1

Severity of the Situation

This is something you can only determine by gathering information either from users or user managers. I know, I know, it means you have to actually talk to people. However, it is a great indicator of whether you should immediately drop everything else and work on this immediately, or if it can wait until the task you're working on is completed. If you don't already, you may want to consider having a written SLA (Service-Level Agreement) that states how quickly you or your team is expected (or required) to react to certain events. Severity should be a key piece of that document.

Relative Effort

If this is a several-thousand-line-of-code object, just shake your head sadly and walk away. Just kidding! However, the effort to just understand what is going on will be significant, let alone the effort to actually fix the performance issues. This is where great documentation comes into play, but it's unlikely that if you're reading this book, you have that kind of help at your disposal.

Additionally, you need to think about QA (quality assurance) effort. The best scenario is to never EVER let untested code go into production. By untested, I mean code that hasn't passed a rigorous QA process. Running something once on your laptop seems like a great idea, but there are all sorts of weird scenarios that you may not be aware of, that a QA professional will have a much better grasp on.

How many precise pain points are in this code? This will be the biggest determination of what kind of triage we can perform to put smiles on the users' faces (or at least make them stop complaining to your boss). Regardless of any of these answers though, if code has been identified as a real problem, triage is only your first step. Even if you "fix" it with an index or other smooth wizardry, DO NOT STOP there! Fully document the code and rewrite if necessary.

Problem Areas

"Hello? Sam DBA? Every time a user tries to change their display name, the application hangs for seconds, and it's really frustrating everyone."

The best way to see what's going on with code is to go run some of the code that is causing problems. Sometimes, settings outside of the actual SQL code can cause issues as well. Application connection strings can sometimes set ANSI settings, and this can make SQL code run very differently from SQL Server Management Studio (SSMS), for example. We're going to assume that this has already been ruled out and isn't the cause of what we're seeing in this book, but I wanted you to be aware that if you haven't checked into those possibilities, you probably should.

This is really useful information that you just received from the caller. Be aware, however, that people like to throw around terms like "always" and "never" pretty lightly. Try to get details: "When you say every time, is it 100% of the time? Is it 90% of the time? Is it any time of day or limited to certain times?" Document the answers to go along with the ticket/request/complaint documentation.

Let's go look at what's happening when a user tries to change their display name. We're going to try to change the following users' display names in the sections to follow as we look for where the issues are. We'll use Jon Skeet who has an Id of 22656 and stic who has an Id of 31996. The query will be run against the dbo.Users table.

STATISTICS IO and Time

STATISTICS IO is a measure of the amount of IO resources a query uses, and STATISTICS TIME measures CPU and elapsed time a query runs, as well as query compile time. If you are counting on that number at the bottom right of SSMS to measure query time, STOP IT! It is not accurate – or certainly not accurate ENOUGH.

Query Window Setup

First, open up SSMS. Connect to the database and open a new query window and then turn STATISTICS IO and STATISTICS TIME on. To do this through the UI, choose the menu option for Query, then Query Options, and then Advanced. Figure 1-1 shows the Advanced window for the Query Options.

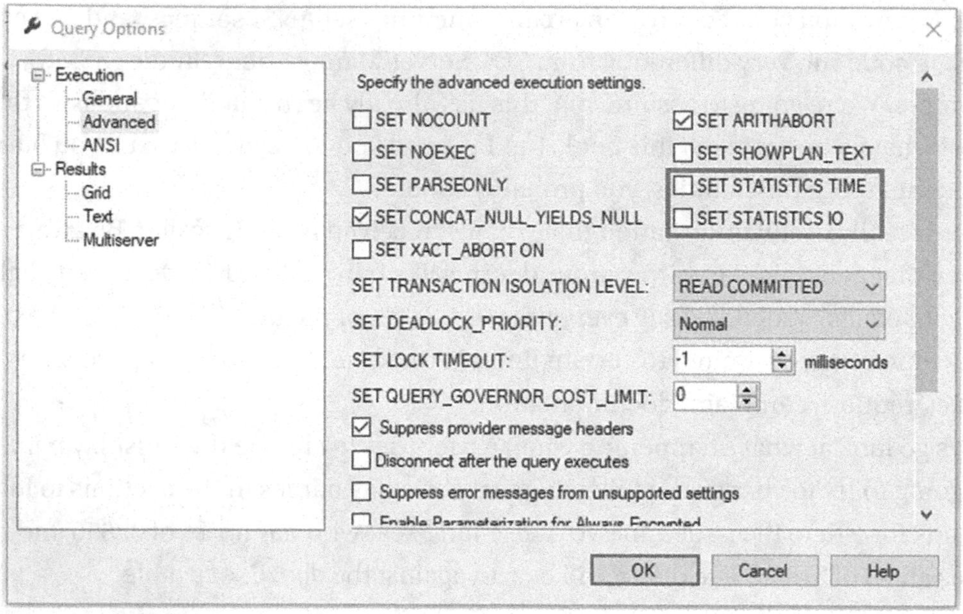

Figure 1-1. *Query Options Advanced window in SSMS*

Make sure you check BOTH the SET STATISTICS TIME and the SET STATISTICS IO boxes and then click OK.

If you want to go all scripting, you simply type in the query window the code shown in Listing 1-1.

Listing 1-1. Command to set STATISTICS TIME and IO on

```
SET STATISTICS TIME, IO ON;
```

and click Execute (or hit Ctrl-E). Please note that either way you set STATISTICS TIME and IO on, it will only be set for that specific query window or connection (SPID). If the connection gets reset (e.g., restarting SSMS) or if you open another query window, you will need to turn STATISTICS TIME and IO on again for the new query window.

Code Tests

Next, we want to update a user's name. So, first, I went and found a user by querying the Users table and came up with a quick query to change a name. I ran it twice, because the first run usually includes compile time. This user's original name was "stic", by the way. We'll change it back later.

Listing 1-2. Code to update the display name of user "stic"

```
UPDATE Users
SET DisplayName = 'stic in mud'
WHERE Id = 31996;
```

Listing 1-3 shows what the STATISTICS IO and TIME output looks like for the query in Listing 1-2.

Listing 1-3. SSMS STATISTICS TIME and IO output

```
SQL Server parse and compile time:
   CPU time = 0 ms, elapsed time = 0 ms.
SQL Server parse and compile time:
   CPU time = 0 ms, elapsed time = 0 ms.
Table 'Users'. Scan count 0, logical reads 3, physical reads 0, read-ahead
reads 0, lob logical reads 0, lob physical reads 0, lob read-ahead reads 0.
SQL Server parse and compile time:
   CPU time = 0 ms, elapsed time = 0 ms.
 SQL Server Execution Times:
   CPU time = 0 ms,  elapsed time = 0 ms.
Table 'WidePosts'. Scan count 1, logical reads 61083, physical reads 0,
read-ahead reads 0, lob logical reads 0, lob physical reads 0, lob read-
ahead reads 0.
 SQL Server Execution Times:
   CPU time = 110 ms,  elapsed time = 116 ms.
Table 'WidePosts'. Scan count 1, logical reads 305110, physical reads 0,
read-ahead reads 0, lob logical reads 0, lob physical reads 0, lob read-
ahead reads 0.
 SQL Server Execution Times:
   CPU time = 1141 ms,  elapsed time = 1142 ms.
 SQL Server parse and compile time:
   CPU time = 1141 ms,  elapsed time = 1142 ms.

 SQL Server Execution Times:
   CPU time = 0 ms,  elapsed time = 0 ms.
SQL Server Execution Times:
   CPU time = 0 ms,  elapsed time = 0 ms.
```

```
SQL Server Execution Times:
   CPU time = 1266 ms,  elapsed time = 1270 ms.
```

There is a much nicer way to look at the output in Listing 1-3. Go to the web site http://statisticsparser.com/, and paste that output into the big window. Click the Parse button, and scroll to the bottom of the page. You'll get a nice summary table that will give you what you need to know at a glance. This is the section labeled "Totals" on the web page. Table 1-1 shows the read columns from the "Totals" section after running the output shown in Listing 1-3 through the Statistics Parser web site.

Table 1-1. *The "Totals" section read columns of the Statistics Parser site output for Listing 1-3*

Table	Scan Count	Logical Reads	Physical Reads	Read-Ahead Reads
Total	2	366,195	0	0
Users	0	3	0	0
WidePosts	2	366,192	0	0

	CPU	Elapsed
SQL Server parse and compile time:	00:00:01.141	00:00:01.142
SQL Server Execution Times:	00:00:02.532	00:00:02.539
Total	**00:00:03.673**	**00:00:03.681**

So what are we looking at with Table 1-1? When we're using STATISTICS output to help with query tuning, we're mostly going to focus on logical reads. The first time you run a query, if your data isn't in memory, you will see higher physical reads. When testing queries, I generally ignore the first run and focus on the second. This is more accurate to what is usually seen in production, where the data being called frequently will already be in memory. Also, by always using this method, we can make sure we're comparing apples to apples.

We are seeing a LOT of page reads in Table 1-1, especially for the update of a single row. But what is this WidePosts table? We weren't updating that table… were we? No, we were updating the dbo.Users table. Somehow, this WidePosts table is related to the Users table. In SSMS, are there any objects around the Users table? A foreign key constraint? A… wait, a trigger? Hmm, let's look at the definition of the trigger, which is shown in Listing 1-4.

Listing 1-4. ALTER statement for the ut_Users_WidePosts trigger

```
/***************************************************************
  Object Description: Pushes user changes to the WidePosts table.
  Revision History:
  Date          Name            Label/PTS    Description
  -----------   --------------  ----------   -------------------
  2019.05.12    LBohm                        Initial Release
****************************************************************/

ALTER TRIGGER [dbo].[ut_Users_WidePosts] ON [dbo].[Users]
FOR UPDATE
AS
SET NOCOUNT ON;

IF EXISTS
(
    SELECT 1
    FROM INSERTED i
    INNER JOIN dbo.WidePosts wp ON i.id = wp.OwnerUserId
)
BEGIN
    IF EXISTS
    (
        SELECT 1
        FROM INSERTED i
        INNER JOIN dbo.WidePosts wp ON i.Id = wp.OwnerUserId
        WHERE i.Age <> wp.Age
```

```
                    OR i.CreationDate <> wp.UserCreationDate
                    OR i.DisplayName <> wp.DisplayName
                    OR i.DownVotes <> wp.DownVotes
                    OR i.EmailHash <> wp.EmailHash
                    OR i.[Location] <> wp.[Location]
                    OR i.Reputation <> wp.Reputation
                    OR i.UpVotes <> wp.UpVotes
                    OR i.[Views] <> wp.[Views]
                    OR i.WebsiteUrl <> wp.WebsiteUrl
        )
    BEGIN
        UPDATE wp
        SET
        wp.[AboutMe] = LEFT(i.AboutMe, 2000)
                , wp.[Age] = i.Age
                , wp.[UserCreationDate] = i.CreationDate
                , wp.[DisplayName] = i.DisplayName
                , wp.[DownVotes] = i.DownVotes
                , wp.[EmailHash] = i.EmailHash
                , wp.[LastAccessDate] = i.LastAccessDate
                , wp.[Location] = i.[Location]
                , wp.[Reputation] = i.Reputation
                , wp.[UpVotes] = i.UpVotes
                , wp.[Views] = i.[Views]
                , wp.[WebsiteUrl] = i.WebsiteUrl
                , wp.AccountID = i.AccountID
        FROM dbo.WidePosts wp
        INNER JOIN INSERTED i ON wp.OwnerUserId = i.Id
        WHERE i.Age <> wp.Age
                OR i.CreationDate <> wp.UserCreationDate
                OR i.DisplayName <> wp.DisplayName
                OR i.DownVotes <> wp.DownVotes
                OR i.EmailHash <> wp.EmailHash
                OR i.[Location] <> wp.[Location]
                OR i.Reputation <> wp.Reputation
```

```
            OR i.UpVotes <> wp.UpVotes
            OR i.[Views] <> wp.[Views]
            OR i.WebsiteUrl <> wp.WebsiteUrl;
        END;
END;
GO
```

Huh. Every time we are updating the Users table, it sends the update to any records in this WidePosts table where the OwnerUserID is equal to the Users table id. It's doing a LOT of reads to perform this task. Let's run another example, and this time we'll grab an execution plan.

Execution Plans

An execution plan shows how SQL Server decided to run your query or statement. It shows the operators that the optimizer chose. If you have never looked at one, it can be confusing. The execution plan is XML data that can be parsed into a diagram of what operators the SQL Server engine uses to fulfill your query request. (Well, that's clear as mud, right?) When a query is run, SQL Server uses the Query Optimizer to figure out the best way to return data or perform the request. For each table that we're getting data from or performing an operation against, SQL Server will use one or more operators to access that table. For example, if we need data from a large portion of the Posts table, SQL Server will perform a "table scan" – that is, it will read all of the data pages for the table – to find the data to return. The plan will also show how many rows SQL Server is expecting to push along to the next operator.

The first things I look for at a quick glance are big fat lines (indicating a LOT of data, or number of rows being pushed to the next operator). Also, I review which operators show the most work being done. I use Plan Explorer to help sort operations by the work being done per operation, which allows us to easily find the most expensive culprits. So how do we get this information?

In SSMS, there is a button you can click above the query window. When you hover over it, it will show you text reading "Get Actual Execution Plan". This icon is shown in Figure 1-2, surrounded by a box.

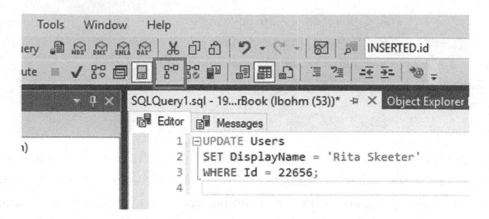

Figure 1-2. *Turning on an actual execution plan in SSMS*

Statistics

An actual execution plan is simply an estimated execution plan including statistics information, so generally they're not very different. Statistics are metadata that SQL Server keeps against columns in tables to indicate the distribution of data. In a dictionary, for example, there are lots of words starting with the letters "st". There are less words starting with "zy". This skew of data is tracked through statistics, which helps the Query Optimizer find a better plan.

I usually use an actual execution plan because it's also an easy way to see if statistics might be out of date and require maintenance. If we get back a single row and the Query Optimizer thinks we're returning 3,000 rows, statistics maintenance might be needed.

Let's run a query updating a different display name now.

Listing 1-5. Updating the display name for user ID 22656

```
UPDATE Users
SET DisplayName = 'Rita Skeeter'
WHERE Id = 22656;
```

What can our execution plan tell us? Let's take a look at the plan generated by running the code in Listing 1-5. If you have SentryOne Plan Explorer installed, you can right-click the execution plan in SSMS (look for the tab near your Results tab) and choose to open the plan in Plan Explorer from the menu that appears.

Once you look at the execution plan in Plan Explorer, you'll see something similar to what we see in Figure 1-3. Please make sure you have clicked the third row of the Results tab Statement output – we want to be looking at the query plan for the most expensive (highest estimated cost) part of the query we ran.

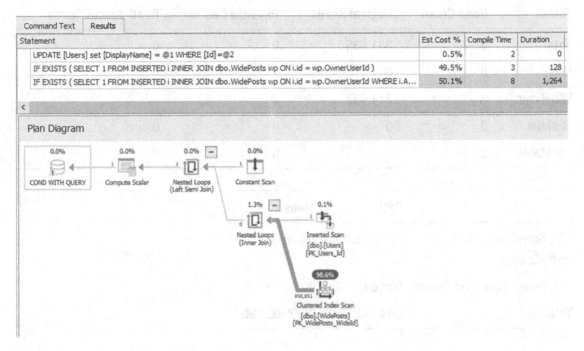

Figure 1-3. *Initial execution plan for the query in Listing 1-5*

We see that the most effort was spent on a clustered index scan for WidePosts, since the trigger updates the WidePosts table when the Users table is updated.

What is a clustered index scan? Well, a clustered index is the index where all of the table's data is stored, in the order specified by the index. There can only be a single clustered index per table. If a table does not have a clustered index, it is considered a heap. So a scan of the clustered index is comparable to a scan of the entire table.

Also, there are a lot of rows being read in that operation. Well, if we decided to look in the WidePosts table, we'd find that there were 4,394 rows of data that included the OwnerUserID corresponding to user ID 22656. That's all well and good, but we are reading over 850,000 rows. (We can see that 850,000 rows in Figure 1-3; it's the number right under the wide arrow leading from the Clustered Index Scan.) This is a problem that we will need to address.

The STATISTICS IO and TIME output is very similar, as we can see in Table 1-2.

Table 1-2. *The "Totals" section read columns of the Statistics Parser site output for the code in Listing 1-5*

Table	Scan Count	Logical Reads	Physical Reads	Read-Ahead Reads
Total	**3**	**341,935**	**2**	**0**
Users	0	3	2	0
WidePosts	3	341,932	0	0
Workfile	0	0	0	0
Worktable	0	0	0	0

	CPU	Elapsed
SQL Server parse and compile time:	00:00:00.000	00:00:00.001
SQL Server Execution Times:	00:00:02.780	00:00:02.789
Total	**00:00:02.780**	**00:00:02.790**

Perform Triage if Possible

Is There an Index?

The answer is that there is no index on the OwnerUserID in the WidePosts table. If we could add one, maybe we wouldn't need to scan the entire table to find the records we need to change. The join from INSERTED (the trigger inserted table) to WidePosts was just on the OwnerUserID, so that's the only column we're going to index, as shown in the index create statement in Listing 1-6.

Listing 1-6. CREATE statement for index on WidePosts table

```
IF NOT EXISTS (SELECT 1
    FROM sys.indexes
```

```
    WHERE object_id = OBJECT_ID('dbo.WidePosts')
        AND name="ix_Posts_ownerUserID")
BEGIN
CREATE NONCLUSTERED INDEX IX_WidePosts_OwnerUserID
  ON dbo.WidePosts (OwnerUserID);
END;
GO
```

Let's go look to see if there is a change when we run queries to change the user names back to what they were. We'll start with the first user, whose original name was "stic", and use the update statement shown in Listing 1-7.

Listing 1-7. Reset of user display name for "stic"

```
UPDATE Users
SET DisplayName = 'stic'
WHERE Id = 31996;
```

After we run the STATISTICS IO and TIME output through statisticsparser.com, we see results that look like the results shown in Table 1-3.

Table 1-3. *Totals for STATISTICS IO and TIME for an indexed UPDATE*

Table	Scan Count	Logical Reads	Physical Reads	Read-Ahead Reads
Total	2	41	0	0
Users	0	3	0	0
WidePosts	2	38	0	0

	CPU	Elapsed
SQL Server parse and compile time:	00:00:00.000	00:00:00.000
SQL Server Execution Times:	00:00:00.000	00:00:00.000
Total	**00:00:00.000**	**00:00:00.000**

That looks much more like what we were expecting to see. There was only one row affected though. How would this translate into the second query we ran, which involved updating about 4,400 rows? Let's take a look by running the code in Listing 1-8. First, though, go ahead and toggle capturing the actual execution plan if it isn't already on, so we can also review that as well.

Listing 1-8. Update user with many WidePosts rows

```
UPDATE Users
SET DisplayName = 'Jon Skeet'
WHERE Id = 22656;
```

The output for the STATISTICS IO and TIME is shown in Table 1-4.

Table 1-4. *STATISTICS IO and TIME output for user update with many WidePosts rows*

Table	Scan Count	Logical Reads	Physical Reads	Read-Ahead Reads
Total	3	35,467	0	0
Users	0	9	0	0
WidePosts	3	35,458	0	0
Worktable	0	0	0	0

	CPU	Elapsed
SQL Server parse and compile time:	00:00:00.000	00:00:00.001
SQL Server Execution Times:	00:00:00.376	00:00:00.456
Total	**00:00:00.376**	**00:00:00.457**

There are a lot more logical reads in the output in Table 1-4 than we see in Table 1-3, because we're finding 4,400 rows instead of 1; that makes a lot of sense. When we look at the execution plan, shown here in Figure 1-4, we see how our index affected the operators chosen to fulfill this query.

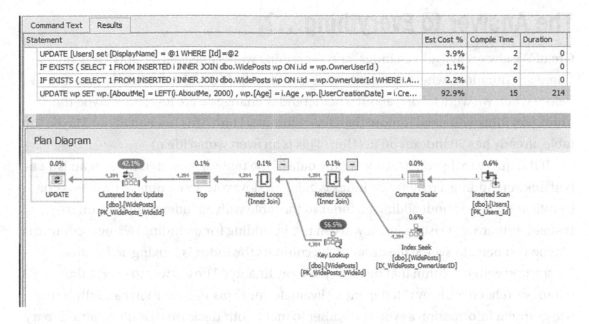

Figure 1-4. *Execution plan for user name change query after indexing*

Excellent! For the line with the highest estimated cost, we don't see a clustered index scan anymore. A significant percentage of the work being done in this trigger is now the actual update of the WidePosts table. There is a key lookup; we could potentially eliminate this by adding included columns to our index. However, with the fact that we're now sub-second for even users with a lot of records, we can probably stop here since we have cut out most of the extra work that SQL Server was doing.

Risk Level of the Change

Index changes are low-risk changes if the following things are true:

- The index is narrow (it contains few columns, and the column datatypes are small).

- There aren't an excessive number of indexes on the table.

In this case, we see a very low-risk code change (single-column index to a table with only a clustered index and one other nonclustered index) for a very big benefit when adding the index in Listing 1-6.

The Answer to Everything…?

Great! We always just add an index, and everything works magically, right? Well, no. There are situations where you don't want to add an index, which we briefly mentioned before when we were talking about whether index changes were low risk. Maybe the index you think you need is more than ten columns. (Hint: This is a bad idea.) Maybe the table already has 30 indexes on it. (Hint: This is an even worse idea.)

If the query really requires a lot of the data in the table, a clustered index scan isn't a bad answer. Adding a really wide index is going to slow your write times down, possibly significantly. How about adding an index to the table with 30 indexes already on it? Instead, is there an existing index you can use by adding (or including) a single column? Maybe you need to switch the order of the columns the index is looking at, because it's starting with a column that has really low cardinality? The answer to everything database-related is always "It depends." Evaluate your specific situation carefully and use as much information as you can gather to make your decisions. Don't be afraid to try something to see if it's going to work. Please do that in a test environment first though!

For those of you who don't recognize the term "cardinality," it indicates the number of different values a column can contain. For example, a bit column can have three different possible values. (Okay, you anti-NULL people out there, you hush. This is just an example…) The values would be 0, 1, or NULL, if you allow it to be NULL able (yes, yes, I heard you the first time). Let's say we have a 1,000,000-row table. There would be a lot of rows with each value. On the other hand, if the column is a datetime column and it gets populated with the date/time a record was added, each value would presumably be different. The bit column would be said to have "low" cardinality (the column contains many equivalent values), whereas the datetime column would be said to have "high" cardinality (the column contains many different values).

Triage Outside of Indexing

What are some other scenarios? I have seen objects (often triggers and stored procedures) that updated a separate table, but it was NOT able to use an index on the linking column even though it existed. Because there were multiple inequivalent statements in the WHERE clause, an index might not be used, which could cause blocking.

If Possible, Queries Should Join on Key Values

In order to make the most effective use of constraints like foreign keys, it's best if queries can join on these key values. In this case, we would also want to make sure the foreign key columns were indexed as well to help SQL Server be able to quickly find the data it needs. Sometimes this can be helped by adding a temporary table to pull data that we need to check against, doing our checks, and then using the key value from that temporary table to join back to the table to perform updates or deletes.

SARGability

A statement is said to be "SARGable" – which stands for Search ARGument – if the JOIN and WHERE clause statements allow indexes to be used. We will go much more in-depth on this later in the book, but for now just be aware that sometimes there may be simple rewrites to make a query SARGable where it hasn't been before.

Summary

Triage can also be done on any object type; for these examples, we were focusing on a trigger, but the same logic applies to the different objects – functions, stored procedures, views, or any other SQL Server object. Indexes are usually low-risk changes and can be very effective at Band-Aiding code. Reviewing queries to see if the joins are on key values can also help performance by taking advantage of foreign key constraints. Small rewrites of queries can also be effective if they allow queries to use indexes that they couldn't formerly use.

Once you have performed triage, it's time to dig deeper into the object, document any possible problem areas, and evaluate for a thorough rewrite.

CHAPTER 2

Documentation

Poorly performing code should be thoroughly documented before we undertake a rewrite. It is easy to start grabbing and rewriting code only to get bogged down in nested if statements, while loops, or calls to other SQL objects. If we have an understanding of the desired functionality, as well, we can make the determination whether the current code should be refactored or if we should just start from scratch.

Incorporating Existing Documentation

We can start with the code. If we don't have any additional documentation, we're going to need to figure out the functionality from the code itself. We should absolutely record our starting point for the code as well, for reference. Hopefully you're using some sort of versioning software, but we also want the information quick at hand for easy access. For this chapter, we're going to look at a report stored procedure that is running for days, that does a daily tally of some data across a month. It took me 45 minutes to run this stored procedure for the month of August 2012; be aware of that if you choose to follow along with the book and run the examples. Let's take a look at what the code to alter this stored procedure contains; we can see it here in Listing 2-1.

Listing 2-1. DailySummaryReportPerMonth stored procedure code

```
/********************************************************************
Description: Data for daily report for a month
--Test call:
-- EXECUTE dbo.DailySummaryReportPerMonth @monthYear = '20180801';
    2019.05.26      LBohm           INITIAL RELEASE
********************************************************************/
```

L. Bohm, *Refactoring Legacy T-SQL for Improved Performance*, https://doi.org/10.1007/978-1-4842-5581-0_2

```
ALTER PROCEDURE [dbo].[DailySummaryReportPerMonth] @monthYear DATETIME
AS
BEGIN
    /* in case the first day of the month not passed in */
    SET @monthYear = DATEADD(month, DATEDIFF(month, 0, @monthYear), 0);

DECLARE @postID             INT
    , @dayOfMonth           TINYINT
    , @numAnswers           INT
    , @numUsers             INT
    , @acceptedAnswerID     INT
    , @userID               INT
    , @displayName          NVARCHAR(40)
    , @isAccepted           BIT
    , @userCtThisPost       SMALLINT
    , @numUpvotes           SMALLINT;

CREATE TABLE #finalOutput
    ( monthyear                         DATETIME
    , dayOfMonth                        TINYINT
    , dayOfWeek                         TINYINT
    , numPosts                          SMALLINT
    , numResponses                      SMALLINT
    , numUsersResponded                 SMALLINT
    , highNumUsersSinglePost            SMALLINT
    , userMostResponses                 NVARCHAR(40) -- DisplayName
    , percentagePosts                   DECIMAL(8, 7)
    , numHighestUpvotesOneAnswer SMALLINT
    );
DECLARE @usersDay TABLE
    ( dayOfMonth            TINYINT
    , userID                INT
    , displayName           NVARCHAR(40)
    , numPostsAnswered      SMALLINT
    , numAcceptedAnsPosts SMALLINT
    );
```

```
/* get first post in the time period that isn't a comment or answer */
SET @postID = COALESCE(
        (
            SELECT MIN(Id)
            FROM dbo.Posts
            WHERE DATEADD(month, DATEDIFF(month, 0, creationDate), 0)
            = @monthYear
                AND PostTypeId = 1
    ), 0);

        /* get all posts in the time period that aren't comments or
        answers */

WHILE @postID > 0
        BEGIN
        SELECT @numAnswers = p.AnswerCount
                , @acceptedAnswerid = p.AcceptedAnswerId
                , @dayOfMonth = DATEPART(dd, p.CreationDate)
        FROM dbo.Posts p
        WHERE p.Id = @postID;

        IF EXISTS
            (
                SELECT 1
                FROM #finalOutput
                WHERE dayOfMonth = @dayOfMonth
            )
            BEGIN
            -- update
            UPDATE fo
            SET fo.numPosts = fo.numPosts + 1
                    , fo.numResponses = fo.numResponses + @numAnswers
            FROM #finalOutput fo
            WHERE fo.dayOfMonth = @dayOfMonth;
            END;
            ELSE
```

```
            BEGIN
            -- insert
            INSERT INTO #finalOutput
                    ( monthYear
                    , dayOfMonth
                    , dayOfWeek
                    , numPosts
                    , numResponses
                    , numUsersResponded
                    , highNumUsersSinglePost
                    , userMostResponses
                    , numHighestUpvotesOneAnswer
                    )
            VALUES
                    ( @monthYear
                    , @dayOfMonth
                    , DATEPART(dw, DATEADD(dd, @dayOfMonth - 1, @monthYear))
                    , 1
                    , @numAnswers
                    , 0
                    , 0
                    , "
                    , 0
                    );
        END;

        /*  now the user stuff */
    SET @userCtThisPost = 0;
    SET @userID = COALESCE(
        (
                SELECT MIN(p.ownerUserId)
                FROM dbo.Posts p
                WHERE p.ParentId = @postID
                            AND p.PostTypeId = 2
        ), 0);
    WHILE @userID > 0
```

```
BEGIN
SET @isAccepted = COALESCE(
        (
                SELECT 1
                FROM dbo.Posts p
                WHERE p.OwnerUserId = @userID
                        AND p.ParentId = @postID
                        AND p.Id = @acceptedAnswerID
        ), 0);
SET @userCtThisPost = @userCtThisPost + 1;
SET @numUpvotes = COALESCE(
        (
                SELECT MAX(p.Score)
                FROM dbo.Posts p
                WHERE p.OwnerUserId = @userID
                        AND p.ParentId = @postID
        ), 0);
UPDATE fo
SET fo.numUsersResponded = fo.numUsersResponded + 1
        , fo.numHighestUpvotesOneAnswer = CASE
                WHEN @numUpvotes > fo.numHighestUpvotesOneAnswer
                THEN @numUpvotes
                ELSE fo.numHighestUpvotesOneAnswer
                END
FROM #finalOutput fo
WHERE fo.dayOfMonth = @dayOfMonth;

/* add records to user table for later calculations */
        IF EXISTS
                (
                        SELECT 1
                        FROM @usersDay
                        WHERE dayOfMonth = @dayOfMonth
                                        AND userID = @userID
                )
                BEGIN
```

```
            UPDATE ud
            SET ud.numPostsAnswered = ud.numPostsAnswered + 1
                    , ud.numAcceptedAnsPosts = ud.numAcceptedAnsPosts +
                        @isAccepted
            FROM @usersDay ud
            WHERE dayOfMonth = @dayOfMonth
                    AND userID = @userID;
            END;
            ELSE
            BEGIN
            INSERT INTO @usersDay
                    ( dayOfMonth
                    , userID
                    , displayName
                    , numPostsAnswered
                    , numAcceptedAnsPosts
                    )
            SELECT @dayOfMonth
                    , @userID
                    , u.DisplayName
                    , 1
                    , @isAccepted
            FROM dbo.Users u
            WHERE u.Id = @userID;
            END;
        SET @userID = COALESCE(
            (
                    SELECT MIN(p.OwnerUserId)
                    FROM dbo.Posts p
                    WHERE p.ParentId = @postID
                        AND PostTypeId = 2
                        AND p.OwnerUserId > @userID
```

```
                    ), 0);
                END;
        UPDATE fo
        SET fo.highNumUsersSinglePost = CASE
                        WHEN @userCtThisPost > fo.highNumUsersSinglePost
                        THEN @userCtThisPost
                    ELSE fo.highNumUsersSinglePost
                        END
        FROM #finalOutput fo
        WHERE fo.dayOfMonth = @dayOfMonth;

        /* get next post ID */
        SET @postID = COALESCE(
            (
                    SELECT MIN(Id)
                    FROM dbo.Posts
                    WHERE DATEADD(month, DATEDIFF(month, 0, creationDate), 0)
                    = @monthYear
                        AND PostTypeId = 1
                        AND Id > @postID
            ), 0);
        END;
/* final day user calculations */
UPDATE fo
SET fo.userMostResponses =
    (
            SELECT ud.displayName
            FROM @usersDay ud
            WHERE ud.dayOfMonth = fo.dayOfMonth
                AND ud.numPostsAnswered =
            (
                    SELECT MAX(udm.numPostsAnswered)
                    FROM @usersDay udm
                    WHERE ud.dayOfMonth = fo.dayOfMonth
            )
```

```
    )
    , fo.percentagePosts = CASE
                WHEN fo.numPosts = 0
                THEN 0
                ELSE CAST(
                    (
                        SELECT MAX(ud.numPostsAnswered)
                        FROM @usersDay ud
                        WHERE ud.dayOfMonth = fo.dayOfMonth
                    ) / fo.numPosts AS DECIMAL(8, 7))
                END
FROM #finalOutput fo;

SELECT *
FROM #finalOutput;

END;
```

Functionality Documentation

We're fortunate enough to have information on what this report is supposed to do! We have a user story that lists the requirements. Remember this database is a backup of the StackOverflow database, which contains programming questions from users, answers to those questions, and comments both on the initial posts and answers to those posts.

The functional requirements are given in this user story:

For each day in a given month, I need to know

1. How many questions were posted?

2. How many answers to those questions were posted, regardless of date?

3. How many unique users answered those posts?

4. What is the highest amount of distinct users that responded to a single question in that month?

5. Which user responded to the most questions posted in that month?

6. How many questions did that user respond to?

7. What percentage of the overall questions posted in that month was that?

8. How many of those responses were marked as accepted answers?

Having access to the functional requirements (in this case, our user story) is an excellent start. As we work through rewriting this code once we have the documentation complete, we can break it down into much smaller pieces and not only focus on the performance of each piece but verify that it is satisfying the functionality requirements.

Statistics Information and Execution Plans

In most cases, both the STATISTICS TIME and IO output, as well as an execution plan, should also be captured and included in the documentation. In this case, however, it is virtually impossible to capture without writing a novel instead of code documentation. The original code contains two nested while loops, which makes for ungainly STATISTICS output as well as a massive execution plan. Both the STATISTICS output and the execution plan will need to show a section for each piece of each loop, making the output excessive.

Coding (Anti) Patterns

Here is a checklist of coding patterns that should be examined closely, because they could lead to red flags:

- Multiple calls to a single table

- Datatypes: Mismatches between parameters and database fields, field width

- Subqueries: Number and location (clause of the query)

- Calculations

- Temporary tables and table variables

- Loops and/or cursors

- CTEs (common table expressions)

- Join types used

- Use of LIKE, NOT LIKE, or NOT IN

- DISTINCT, TOP, or other sorting operations

- Calls to other SQL objects (stored procedures, views, functions)

- Other anomalies

Number of Calls to Each Database Table

I like to start the anti-pattern section of the documentation with a table that has the name of each database table being called. As we go through the code, we can add an additional record under each table so we can see at a glance how often a single table has been touched by the code. I also include information on filtering used for each call. We will note calls to temporary tables and table variables as well. Table 2-1 shows the documentation of table calls for the stored procedure shown in Listing 2-1.

Table 2-1. *Documentation of number of calls per table for Listing 2-1*

Table	Operation	Columns Returned	Filtering
dbo.Posts	Select	MIN(Id)	CreationDate, PostTypeId
	Select	AnswerCount, AcceptedAnswerId, CreationDate	Id
	Select	MIN(OwnerUserId)	ParentId, PostTypeId
	Select	1	OwnerUserId, ParentId, Id
	Select	MAX(Score)	OwnerUserId, ParentId
	Select	MIN(Id)	CreationDate, PostTypeId, Id
	Select	MIN(OwnerUserId)	ParentId, PostTypeId, OwnerUserId

(continued)

Table 2-1. (*continued*)

Table	Operation	Columns Returned	Filtering
#finalOutput	Exists		dayOfMonth
	Insert or update	Row OR numPosts, numResponses	Single record (dayOfMonth)
	Update	numUsersResponded, numHighestUpvotesOneAnswer	Single record (dayOfMonth)
	Update	highNumUsersSinglePost	Single record (dayOfMonth)
	Update	userMostResponses, percentagePosts	Single record (dayOfMonth)
	Select	*	
@usersDay	Exists		Single record (userID/dayOfMonth)
	Insert or update	Row OR numPostsAnswered, numAcceptedAnsPosts	Single record (userID/dayOfMonth)
	Select	displayName	dayOfMonth, numPostsAnswered
	Select	Max(numPostsAnswered)	dayOfMonth
	Select	Max(numPostsAnswered)	dayOfMonth
dbo.Users	Select	DisplayName	Single record (Id)

One thing that stands out immediately is that there are several updates to the #finalOutput temporary table, all based on the same filtering criteria. Also, we're selecting from the database table dbo.Posts quite often.

Datatype Mismatches

In the stored procedure in Listing 2-1, the database field datatypes all match the parameter datatypes or temporary table/table variable field datatypes that are used for filtering criteria. But why does this even matter? Let's look at a few scenarios.

Data Truncation

What if we have a varchar(100) field called `Field100` in a table and we're pulling this data into a field in a temporary table (`Field40`) that is set as a varchar(40) datatype? As long as there is less than 40 characters of data in Field100 in the rows that we're inserting into `Field40` in the temporary table, we should be fine. However, if there are more than 40 characters of data in `Field100` in any of the records to be inserted, we will get a string truncation error upon insert. Let's consider Listing 2-2 which is part 1 of an example of data truncation.

Listing 2-2. Data truncation example part 1

```
DECLARE @sometable TABLE (somecol varchar(40));
DECLARE @othertable TABLE (othercol Varchar(100));

INSERT INTO @othertable(othercol)
VALUES ('blah')
        , ('foo')
        , ('short')
        , ('uhhuh');

INSERT INTO @sometable (somecol)
SELECT othercol
FROM @othertable;

SELECT *
FROM @sometable;
```

When we run the code in Listing 2-2, we get the recordset shown in Table 2-2.

Table 2-2. *Results from the data truncation example part 1*

somecol
blah
foo
short
uhhuh

However, if we run the code for Listing 2-3, which is the second part of the data truncation example, we don't even see a recordset.

Listing 2-3. Data truncation example part 2

```
DECLARE @sometable TABLE (somecol varchar(40));
DECLARE @othertable TABLE (othercol Varchar(100));

INSERT INTO @othertable(othercol)
VALUES ('blah')
        , ('foo')
        , ('short')
        , ('uhhuh')
        , ('nuhuh Im going to be over 40 characters ha');

INSERT INTO @sometable (somecol)
SELECT othercol
FROM @othertable;

SELECT *
FROM @sometable;
```

Instead, under the Messages tab, we see the following:

Listing 2-4. Results from the data truncation example part 2

```
(5 rows affected)
Msg 8152, Level 16, State 14, Line 12
String or binary data would be truncated.
The statement has been terminated.
(0 rows affected)
```

There is nothing quite as frustrating as seeing the error message shown in Listing 2-4 when you have several thousand lines of code, and then need to find the table and column where the truncation is occurring. The stellar folks at Microsoft have added the table and column for this error message in SQL Server 2019, and the angels did sing and the sun did shine through the clouds. However, until you get all of your instances upgraded, you're still going to have to go through the pain of finding code causing truncation the agonizing way.

Implicit Conversion

Microsoft has pretty thorough documentation on datatype conversions, and it's really easy to find. It is on their CAST and CONVERT Books Online page: `https:// docs.microsoft.com/en-us/sql/t-sql/functions/cast-and-convert-transact- sql?view=sql-server-2017`.

There is a big chart that will tell you which datatypes you can convert into what other datatypes. There are pretty dots that indicate where implicit conversion takes place. The chart is nice, but sometimes very difficult to understand. What does this actually mean?

Let's say we have an integer field (`int01`) and we need to compare the value in `int01` to a varchar field (`varchar01`). The field `varchar01` has some integer-type values in it, but of course they are stored as varchars. Listing 2-5 illustrates this with a code example.

Listing 2-5. Implicit conversion example part 1

```
DECLARE @sometable TABLE (int01 INT);
DECLARE @othertable TABLE (varchar01 varchar(8));

INSERT INTO @sometable (int01)
VALUES (1)
          , (10)
          , (23)
          , (47)
          , (56);

INSERT INTO @othertable(varchar01)
VALUES ('23')
          , ('a89')
          , ('56o')
          , ('e1')
          , ('47');

SELECT ot.varchar01
FROM @othertable ot
WHERE EXISTS (SELECT 1
                FROM @sometable st
                WHERE st.int01 = ot.varchar01);
```

Our STATISTICS output from running the code in Listing 2-5 shows that we get a conversion error. This error is shown in Listing 2-6.

Listing 2-6. Conversion error from implicit conversion example part 1

```
Msg 245, Level 16, State 1, Line 21
Conversion failed when converting the varchar value 'a89' to data type int.
```

If we instead run the conversion example in Listing 2-7, we can see evidence of the conversion in the execution plan. (Don't forget to toggle the Execution Plan if you don't have it turned on!)

Listing 2-7. Implicit conversion example part 2

```
DECLARE @sometable TABLE (int01 INT);
DECLARE @othertable TABLE (varchar01 varchar(8));

INSERT INTO @sometable (int01)
VALUES (1)
        , (10)
        , (23)
        , (47)
        , (56);

INSERT INTO @othertable(varchar01)
VALUES ('23')
        , ('89')
        , ('56')
        , ('1')
        , ('47');

SELECT ot.varchar01
FROM @othertable ot
WHERE EXISTS (SELECT 1
              FROM @sometable st
              WHERE st.int01 = ot.varchar01);
```

Once we look at the execution plan for the code in Listing 2-7, which we show in Figure 2-1, we can see a couple of interesting things.

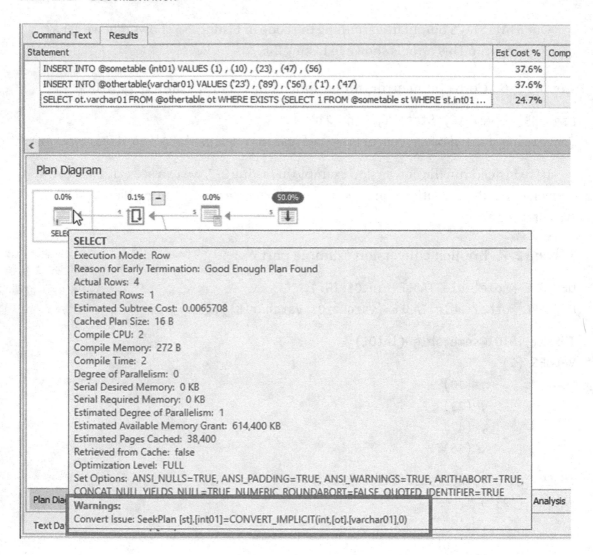

Figure 2-1. *Evidence of implicit conversion*

In Figure 2-1, we see a yellow triangle with an exclamation point on the SELECT operator. If we hover over that operator, there is a pop-up window that has a warning at the bottom. The varchar01 column values were converted to integers to compare against the int01 column values. Let's reread that last sentence and add a little emphasis: SQL Server will implicitly convert ALL OF THE VALUES IN THE VARCHAR01 FIELD – every record in the whole table.

Why would this happen? The answer is, of course, that we (and "we" includes SQL Server) don't know if records are equivalent to other records unless we can compare the values. We have to do a table or index scan so we can first convert ALL THE VALUES in the `varchar01` field to integers so we can determine whether they are equivalent to values in the `int01` field. This will cause a scan instead of a seek, with the corresponding performance overhead of a scan operation.

Field Width

Then there is datatype width. I mean, why not just make everything nvarchar(max) to avoid all of the possible truncation errors and those sorts of things? SQL Server only uses storage space for the number of characters in the field, so it won't matter, right? Well, there are a couple of major concerns with the practice of just setting fields to incorrect datatypes or ridiculous widths.

A serious concern is that people will abuse the practice of setting wide datatypes. You should set every field up to contain only the data that is required. Being thoughtful about using correct datatypes and field widths will avoid the possibility of fields being used as catch-all fields, that people can (and will) use for all sorts of random data. Of course, they will then want to search on that random data....

Another concern is that SQL Server uses something called a memory grant to determine how many resources are needed to run your query. Although SQL Server doesn't store "empty" characters in nvarchar and varchar fields, a memory grant will assume that the width of a row is as wide as that row could possibly be, as opposed to how wide the data in the row actually is. Fields with wide varchars, text, and image datatypes will cause SQL Server's estimate of the memory and tempdb space (and possibly other requirements your query needs) to be very bloated. Then, you have to wait until your SQL Server can find the resources needed to fulfill such grants before it can run your query. I hope you find this situation as frightening to contemplate as I did when I first learned about it....

The upshot to all of this is that datatypes absolutely matter. We'll touch a bit more on datatypes when we get into tables and other objects as well. But in the case of the code in Listing 2-1, whoever wrote this code was very good about checking parameter and temporary object datatypes against the database table datatypes, and there are no datatype concerns for this stored procedure.

Subqueries and Where They're Located

SQL Server is now smart enough (for the most part) to translate subqueries in a SELECT statement to a join. In the past, it used to run each subquery once for each row in the return recordset. Yuck! In a lot of cases that I've seen, though, there will be subquery after subquery that calls almost exactly the same information, from the same table, filtering on the same data. (See? That's why we wanted to capture the filtering data with the table calls.) For example, when we look at the @usersDay calls in the preceding table, we see there are two aggregates both based on the same filtering (dayofmonth). They are both subqueries and will get called as a separate join each if translated by the Query Optimizer to joins. Multiple calls to the same table, whether it's calls in joins or subqueries, are a great target for initial rewrite items, since combining these is usually relatively simple and can significantly reduce reads.

For subqueries in the SELECT statement, we want to look at combining calls to the same table and moving them to some sort of join, usually an OUTER APPLY. When they are in the WHERE clause, we want to look at how we can pull that data out and use it as a join in some way to reduce the hits and reads on those given tables. Complex WHERE clauses can give the optimizer headaches when it is trying to come up with a good query plan; simplifying this logic as much as possible will help it come up with the best plan it can.

The only subqueries in our code in Listing 2-1 are the subqueries calling @usersDay and doing some aggregates. We will note this in our documentation for the stored procedure. Then, when it comes time to rewrite the code, we'll definitely look at combining these subqueries to reduce hits. Yes, we want to do this even for temporary tables and table variables!

Calculations

There can be a lot of gotchas with calculations. Divide-by-zero errors, parentheses causing incorrect results, and even inhibition of parallelism can be found with calculations. Calculations on columns in the WHERE clause can cause table scans just like we saw in implicit conversion earlier in the example in Listing 2-7; if SQL Server needs to determine whether a value in a field is equivalent to a value calculated from another field, it has to perform the calculation on every record to determine if there is equivalence.

Most of the calculations in this stored procedure are very simple, for example, adding one or an integer to a column or variable. Simple calculations aren't generally prone to issues. There is one division calculation at the end, but there is a check to avoid a divide-by-zero error. The code explicitly checks to make sure the divisor is not equal to zero before it performs the calculation, as you can see in the CASE statement, shown again in Listing 2-8.

Listing 2-8. Percentage posts calculation from Listing 2-1

```
CASE
     WHEN fo.numPosts = 0
          THEN 0
     ELSE CAST(
            (
               SELECT MAX(ud.numPostsAnswered)
                  FROM @usersDay ud
                  WHERE ud.dayOfMonth = fo.dayOfMonth
            ) / fo.numPosts AS DECIMAL(8, 7))
          END
```

We are going to want to check all of the database objects this code calls for calculations as well, especially all tables and views. This seems a bit over the top; but there is a good reason. Any reference to a table or view with a computed column which uses a user-defined scalar function will result in a serial plan, even if the column is not referenced in the query. This is a parallelism inhibitor. "But you don't want your queries running parallel, that indicates bad performance!"

This is not exactly true. If a query runs in parallel, it indicates that the cost associated with the query is higher than the cost threshold of parallelism (SQL Server setting). How do they measure this cost? Well, once upon a time there was a computer that a developer used at Microsoft, and a bunch of measurements are tied to this arbitrary standard. We on my team commonly refer to those units as "Mysofts," which generally indicates to us that you can compare them to other ... "things"... but it's not always clear how. But I digress.

If you have a query that is beefy, it's completely okay for it to run parallel. That's why you have multiple CPUs after all, to spread the load for intensive operations. If the query will cost a certain number of Mysofts, you WANT it to run parallel because the elapsed time will be much shorter and your user will be much less grumpy. You do not want some arbitrary mistake by a developer years ago to keep this from being able to happen. So go check your tables and views to make sure there aren't any calculated columns that use a scalar function. In the case of our code in Listing 2-1, there are none.

Temporary Tables and/or Table Variables

We definitely want to document the existence of temporary tables and table variables that appear in whatever code we are documenting: how wide they are, how many changes we make to the data or the definition throughout the procedure, and how many rows we think will be in each. Changing the definition of a temporary table, even if we're adding an index, can cause a recompile of the stored procedure that contains that temporary table. Adding a large amount of data to a temporary table or table variable can also cause a recompile of the containing stored procedure.

What's the difference between temporary tables and table variables anyway? The main difference is that temporary tables have statistics as well as greater indexing support, whereas table variables do not have statistics and can only be indexed in a couple specific ways. We talked briefly about statistics in Chapter 1; here we're specifically referring to data points related to indexes which indicate the distribution of data between each index value. That's why many folks will recommend table variables for a small amount of data (in my opinion, I go with 100 rows or less). Other folks have a different definition of small amount; you may need to determine what works best for you. Another reason for the 100 rows or less recommendation is that the optimizer will assume that a table variable only has one row (again, due to the lack of statistics).

In our stored procedure in Listing 2-1, we have both a table variable and a temporary table. The temporary table #finalOutput is created first and will at most have 31 rows in it (one row for each day of a month). It's made up mostly of smallint columns, although it's got an nvarchar(40) column, a datetime column, a decimal column, and a couple of tinyint columns. This table is quite narrow – it contains only a few columns.

The table variable, @usersDay, is also narrow, but will have many, many more rows – one per user who answers a question on each day. There could be several thousands of rows in @usersDay!

The definitions of both of these objects – @usersDay and #finalOutput – are not changed once created. According to the code, the data will be changing in both many, many times. These changes will occur one row at a time (the adds and updates are all in loops except for the last update for the temporary table).

We'll add the information in Listing 2-9 to the documentation we are creating for the code in Listing 2-1.

Listing 2-9. Table variable and temporary table documentation for code in Listing 2-1

```
#finalOutput temporary table, narrow            max possible rows -  31
      Inserts: one row at a time
      Updates: one row at a time (except last update)
@usersDay table variable, narrow            possible rows - several thousand
      Inserts: one row at a time
      Updates: one row at a time
```

Loops and/or Cursors

The use of loops is where the stored procedure in Listing 2-1 shines; and by that, I mean with an evil red glow. The procedure loops over every post in the time frame of a month and, then within that, loops through every user answering each post. In general, front-end developers think in procedural fashion. Actually, most people think in a procedural fashion. "I do this, then I do that, then I do this, and then I grab the next one and do the same things." Relational databases are meant to work best on batches, but training ourselves to think in terms of batching everything is difficult because so few things in life really work in that manner.

We'll talk much more in depth about concerns with looping as we get into rewriting the code in Listing 2-1, but in terms of documentation we just want to make sure we note everywhere we see row-by-row processing, like we see in the two loops previously mentioned. You'll often hear the acronym RBAR being used to describe code which uses row-by-row processing. The acronym RBAR was coined by Jeff Moden, and stands for "row by agonizing row."

In terms of what to document for the code in Listing 2-1, first we'll get an idea of how many posts were entered per month, which will indicate how many records need to be processed by the first loop. We do that using the code in Listing 2-10.

Listing 2-10. Code to determine number of posts entered per month

```
SELECT COUNT(1) as NumPosts
, DATEPART(year,CreationDate)
, DATEPART(m, CreationDate)
FROM dbo.Posts
WHERE PostTypeId = 1
GROUP BY DATEPART(year,CreationDate),DATEPART(m,CreationDate)
ORDER BY DATEPART(year,CreationDate),DATEPART(m,CreationDate);
```

For the documentation of Listing 2-1, we'll note the following: 1) there is a while loop that runs through all question posts in a month (roughly 50k–150k), and 2) there is a second, inner while loop for each user responding to a post (there are about two users responding to each post).

CTEs

There are no combined table expressions used in the code in Listing 2-1. When we are documenting code, we look for them because people don't always understand that each time a CTE is referred to, it reruns the CTE evaluation code. This can cause a lot more work to be going on in the background than people realize. There are only two times I use CTEs – when attempting to limit view result sets and when I need to use recursion in my code. The stored procedures `sp_codeCallsCascade` and `sp_codeCalledCascade` that are included with this book code are examples of using CTEs for recursion. Recursion, however, is beyond the scope of this book.

Join Types

Standard join types and syntax are used in the code in Listing 2-1. By standard joins and syntax, we mean explicitly declared joins as "INNER JOIN" or "LEFT OUTER JOIN" or other commonly used join types. There are types of join syntax that used to be acceptable that will cause compiler failures in newer versions of SQL Server.

Also, people who don't understand nonstandard joins well may use them and have unintended consequences in the result set, which may not get caught by QA.

LIKE, NOT LIKE, and NOT IN

The IN and LIKE operators can be misused and cause performance problems. There are generally better alternatives to each of them, which is why we want to document their use in any code we are refactoring. We don't see LIKE or NOT LIKE used at all in the code in Listing 2-1, which is good because the use of either LIKE or NOT LIKE can prohibit queries from using indexes.

There is no usage of NOT IN in the code in Listing 2-1 either. Why are we checking for the use of this operator? There used to be a performance advantage of using EXISTS and NOT EXISTS instead of IN and NOT IN, but that has diminished over time and with newer versions of SQL Server. However, NOT IN and NOT EXISTS handle NULL values in different ways – if the source data for the subquery contains a NULL value, the NOT IN will evaluate to FALSE even if the value really doesn't exist. NOT EXISTS will not have the same issue with NULL in the result set; so we still advise using NOT EXISTS over NOT IN.

DISTINCT, TOP, and Other Sorting Operations

Sorting can be expensive in SQL Server. Many operations, such as TOP and DISTINCT, require some sorting, which is why we want to call them out when we find them. MIN and MAX are also sorting operations, even if an explicit order by clause doesn't exist; the values of the field we're taking the MIN or MAX of need to be sorted so we can determine which is the highest or the lowest.

For each loop in the code in Listing 2-1, we're looking for the MIN(Id) of the table we're looping through. In this case, we see

- MIN(Id) from Posts in a time frame

- MIN(OwnerUserId) from Posts based on a ParentId

Other than these two MIN() columns, there are no operations that would indicate sorting underneath the hood.

Calls to Other User-Defined SQL Objects

Fortunately, there are no other SQL objects (besides the dbo.Posts table) called by the stored procedure in Listing 2-1. I have a stored procedure I wrote based on dependencies that SQL Server keeps track of, that can tell you what other objects are dependent on your object (which in most cases translates to objects called by this). I don't have it tracking tables; it will show stored procedures and functions. I have included the stored procedure with this book; it is called sp_codeCallsCascade. It uses system catalog views to determine the dependencies.

You can use this against your code to see what code your object calls, and then what objects those objects call, and... well, and so on. The call is demonstrated in Listing 2-11.

Listing 2-11. Sample call for sp_codeCallsCascade

```
EXECUTE sp_codeCallsCascade @codeName='DailySummaryReportPerMonth',
@rootSchema = 'dbo';
```

Native SQL Server Functions in a WHERE Clause

We just looked for calls to user-defined SQL objects, including functions. However, we also need to look at the use of native SQL Server functions in WHERE clauses. This use needs to be noted because if the function is working on a table field (even ISNULL), it can cause the query in which it used to be unable to use an index. This is a lot like what we discussed with implicit conversion: if we're going to check to see if two values are equal, we're going to have to evaluate the value of every record to determine if the output of the function matches the value against which we're comparing.

Native SQL Server functions in the WHERE clause are found in two places in the code in Listing 2-1. They are found both in the initial populate for the @postID and the additional populate(s) for the @postID variable. It runs for each of the 150k (or so) posts in a month time frame. The code is shown in Listing 2-12.

Listing 2-12. Native SQL Server function in the WHERE clause from Listing 2-1

```
SET @postID = COALESCE((SELECT MIN(Id)
                    FROM dbo.Posts
                    WHERE  DATEADD(m, DATEDIFF(m, 0, CreationDate),0) =
                    @monthYear
```

```
                                    AND PostTypeId = 1)
            ,0);
```

What happens if we run the code similar to Listing 2-12 to get an execution plan as well as with STATISTICS IO and TIME turned on? We can mock up a test example pretty easily, as shown in Listing 2-13.

Listing 2-13. Mock-up test example of native SQL Server function in the WHERE clause

```
DECLARE @monthYear datetime = '20120801'
     , @postID int;

SET @postID = COALESCE((SELECT MIN(Id)
                        FROM dbo.Posts
                        WHERE  DATEADD(m, DATEDIFF(m, 0, CreationDate),0) =
                        @monthYear
                            AND PostTypeId = 1)
            ,0);
SET @postID = COALESCE((SELECT MIN(Id)
                        FROM dbo.Posts
                        WHERE  DATEADD(m, DATEDIFF(m, 0, CreationDate),0) =
                        @monthYear
                            AND PostTypeId = 1
                            AND Id > @postID)
            ,0);
```

We can see the STATISTICS IO and TIME by looking at Listing 2-14.

Listing 2-14. STATISTICS IO and TIME output from running Listing 2-13

```
SQL Server Execution Times:
   CPU time = 0 ms,  elapsed time = 0 ms.
SQL Server parse and compile time:
   CPU time = 15 ms, elapsed time = 16 ms.

 SQL Server Execution Times:
   CPU time = 0 ms,  elapsed time = 0 ms.
```

45

```
Table 'Posts'. Scan count 2, logical reads 4477272, physical reads 8, read-
ahead reads 4496246, lob logical reads 0, lob physical reads 0, lob read-
ahead reads 0.

(1 row affected)


 SQL Server Execution Times:
   CPU time = 43500 ms,  elapsed time = 83520 ms.
Table 'Posts'. Scan count 2, logical reads 12, physical reads 2, read-ahead
reads 0, lob logical reads 0, lob physical reads 0, lob read-ahead reads 0.

(1 row affected)


 SQL Server Execution Times:
   CPU time = 0 ms,  elapsed time = 3 ms.
SQL Server parse and compile time:
   CPU time = 0 ms, elapsed time = 0 ms.

 SQL Server Execution Times:
   CPU time = 0 ms,  elapsed time = 0 ms.
```

Youch! That is an awful lot of reads, which made the initial call really painful. We can see this from the first set of reads from the Table 'Posts' in Listing 2-14; there are 4,477,272 logical reads and 4,496,256 read-ahead reads. Logical reads are the number of pages that were accessed from memory. Read-ahead reads are when SQL Server tries to guess what data will be needed and move that data into the buffer cache if it isn't there already.

We have to read data for each record to determine if the evaluated CreationDate with the DATEADD/DATEDIFF functions applied equals the @monthYear variable! Each subsequent call to the Posts table will be significantly less painful due to the Id filter (where we say that the Id has to be greater than the @postID value). In the second Table 'Posts' line in Listing 2-14, we only see 12 logical reads and no read-ahead reads.

When we look at the execution plans for the code in Listing 2-14, we see the big lines for the first query and then much more reasonable lines for the second set. "Big lines" refer to the very thick arrows we see coming from the Clustered Index Scan operators on the right-hand side of the plan, that then point to the TOP operators. The second query can use the Id for a seek predicate (where we let SQL Server know we only want Ids greater than the @postID we currently have). This allows SQL Server to use an index seek instead of the index scan (look all the way to the right on each; the top plan shows two clustered index scans, whereas the bottom plan shows two clustered index seeks).

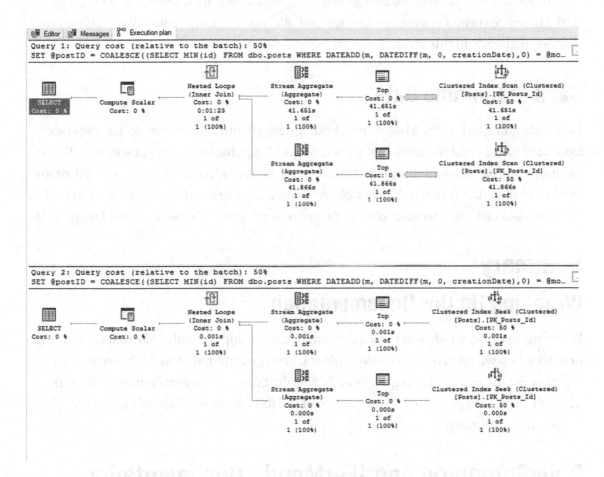

Figure 2-2. Execution plans for queries populating @postID in Listing 2-14

The important message here is to be careful when using scalar functions of any kind (whether user defined or those of the native SQL Server variety) in WHERE clauses against column values!

Indexes

Once we document coding anti-patterns, we should look for indexes that would apply to the query or queries in question. Do we have the correct indexes? We'll use the execution plan to see if those indexes are being used for the query we are examining. If not, why not? There are certain operations that will not allow index usage, some of which we have discussed already in this chapter.

Back to Runtime Data

We're not going to be able to do much about indexes in our documentation of the code from Listing 2-1 until we break that code down and start looking at the pieces of it. With the loops, it's pretty prohibitive to get either aggregates of STATISTICS IO and TIME or an execution plan that is remotely readable. As we get into the rewrite and can start to pull runtime data out, we'll be able to evaluate index usage better, like we did with Listing 2-14.

Summary

Wrapping Up Our Documentation

When we're done, we should have a document containing valuable information that will help us when we go to rewrite the SQL object. The document that we've been putting together for the code in Listing 2-1 is fairly simple; there are very few issues, although those that exist are pretty big. The example of the full documentation of Listing 2-1 follows this summary.

DailySummaryReportPerMonth: Documentation

Code as of 2019.06.02

```
IF NOT EXISTS
(
    SELECT 1
    FROM sys.procedures
    WHERE name = 'DailySummaryReportPerMonth'
```

```
)
BEGIN
     DECLARE @SQL NVARCHAR(1200);
     SET @sQL = N'
/***********************************************************************
    2019.05.26     LBohm              INITIAL STORED PROC STUB CREATE RELEASE
***********************************************************************/

CREATE PROCEDURE dbo.DailySummaryReportPerMonth
AS
     SET NOCOUNT ON;
BEGIN
 SELECT 1;
 END;';
     EXECUTE SP_EXECUTESQL @SQL;
END;
GO


/***********************************************************************
Description: Data for daily report for a month
--Test call:
-- EXECUTE dbo.DailySummaryReportPerMonth @monthYear = '20180801';
    2019.05.26     LBohm              INITIAL RELEASE
***********************************************************************/

ALTER PROCEDURE [dbo].[DailySummaryReportPerMonth] @monthYear DATETIME
AS
     /* in case the first day of the month not passed in */
     SET @monthYear = DATEADD(month, DATEDIFF(month, 0, @monthYear), 0);
     DECLARE @postID          INT
                , @dayOfMonth       TINYINT
                , @numAnswers       INT
                , @numUsers         INT
                , @acceptedAnswerID INT
                , @userID           INT
                , @displayName      NVARCHAR(40)
                , @isAccepted       BIT
```

```
                         , @userCtThisPost      SMALLINT
                         , @numUpvotes          SMALLINT;
CREATE TABLE #finalOutput
( monthYear                    DATETIME
, dayOfMonth                   TINYINT
, dayOfWeek                    TINYINT
, numPosts                     SMALLINT
, numResponses                 SMALLINT
, numUsersResponded            SMALLINT
, highNumUsersSinglePost       SMALLINT
, userMostResponses            NVARCHAR(40) -- DisplayName
, percentagePosts              DECIMAL(8, 7)
, numHighestUpvotesOneAnswer SMALLINT
);
DECLARE @usersDay TABLE
( dayOfMonth          TINYINT
, userID              INT
, displayName         NVARCHAR(40)
, numPostsAnswered    SMALLINT
, numAcceptedAnsPosts SMALLINT
);

/* get first post in the time period that isn't a comment or answer
*/
SET @postID = COALESCE(
(
    SELECT MIN(Id)
    FROM dbo.Posts
    WHERE DATEADD(month, DATEDIFF(month, 0, CreationDate), 0)
    = @monthYear
                    AND postTypeId = 1
), 0);

/* get all posts in the time period that aren't comments or answers
*/
WHILE @postID > 0
BEGIN
```

```
SELECT @numAnswers = p.AnswerCount
            , @acceptedAnswerid = p.AcceptedAnswerId
            , @dayofmonth = DATEPART(dd, p.CreationDate)
FROM dbo.Posts p
WHERE p.Id = @postID;
IF EXISTS
(
    SELECT 1
    FROM #finalOutput
    WHERE dayOfMonth = @dayOfMonth
)
BEGIN
    -- update
    UPDATE fo
        SET fo.numPosts = fo.numPosts + 1
            , fo.numResponses = fo.numResponses +
                @numAnswers
    FROM #finalOutput fo
    WHERE fo.dayOfMonth = @dayOfMonth;
END;
ELSE
BEGIN
    -- insert
    INSERT INTO #finalOutput
    ( monthYear
    , dayOfMonth
    , dayOfWeek
    , numPosts
    , numResponses
    , numUsersResponded
    , highNumUsersSinglePost
    , userMostResponses
    , numHighestUpvotesOneAnswer
    )
    VALUES
            ( @monthYear
```

```
                , @dayOfMonth
                , DATEPART(dw, DATEADD(dd, @dayOfMonth - 1,
                @monthYear))
                , 1
                , @numAnswers
                , 0
                , 0
                , "
                , 0
                );
    END;

    /*  now the user stuff */
    SET @userCtThisPost = 0;
    SET @userID = COALESCE(
    (
        SELECT MIN(p.OwnerUserId)
        FROM dbo.Posts p
        WHERE p.ParentId = @postID
                        AND p.PostTypeId = 2
    ), 0);
    WHILE @userID > 0
    BEGIN
        SET @isAccepted = COALESCE(
        (
            SELECT 1
            FROM dbo.Posts p
            WHERE p.OwnerUserId = @userID
                            AND p.ParentId = @postID
                            AND p.Id = @acceptedAnswerID
        ), 0);
        SET @userCtThisPost = @userCtThisPost + 1;
        SET @numUpvotes = COALESCE(
        (
            SELECT MAX(p.Score)
            FROM dbo.Posts p
```

52

```
                WHERE p.OwnerUserId = @userID
                            AND p.ParentId = @postID
), 0);
UPDATE fo
      SET fo.numUsersResponded = fo.numUsersResponded + 1
      , fo.numHighestUpvotesOneAnswer = CASE
            WHEN @numUpvotes >
            fo.numHighestUpvotesOneAnswer
                THEN @numUpvotes
            ELSE fo.numHighestUpvotesOneAnswer
            END
FROM #finalOutput fo
WHERE fo.dayOfMonth = @dayOfMonth;

/* add records to user table for later calculations */
IF EXISTS
(
      SELECT 1
      FROM @usersDay
      WHERE dayOfMonth = @dayOfMonth
                      AND userID = @userID
)
BEGIN
      UPDATE ud
            SET ud.numPostsAnswered = ud.numPostsAnswered + 1
            , ud.numAcceptedAnsPosts =
              ud.numAcceptedAnsPosts + @isAccepted
      FROM @usersDay ud
      WHERE dayOfMonth = @dayOfMonth
                      AND userID = @userID;
END;
ELSE
BEGIN
      INSERT INTO @usersDay
      ( dayOfMonth
```

```
                        , userID
                        , displayName
                        , numPostsAnswered
                        , numAcceptedAnsPosts
                        )
                                            SELECT @dayOfMonth
                                                        , @userID
                                                        , u.displayName
                                                        , 1
                                                        , @isAccepted
                                            FROM dbo.Users u
                                            WHERE u.Id = @userID;
            END;
            SET @userID = COALESCE(
            (
                    SELECT MIN(p.OwnerUserId)
                    FROM dbo.Posts p
                    WHERE p.ParentId = @postID
                                    AND p.PostTypeId = 2
                                    AND p.OwnerUserId > @userID
            ), 0);
        END;
        UPDATE fo
            SET
            fo.highNumUsersSinglePost = CASE
                    WHEN @userCtThisPost > fo.highNumUsersSinglePost
                            THEN @userCtThisPost
            ELSE fo.highNumUsersSinglePost
                    END
        FROM #finalOutput fo
        WHERE fo.dayOfMonth = @dayOfMonth;

        /* get next post ID */
        SET @postID = COALESCE(
        (
                SELECT MIN(Id)
```

```
            FROM dbo.Posts
            WHERE DATEADD(month, DATEDIFF(month, 0, CreationDate), 0)
            = @monthYear
                                AND PostTypeId = 1
                                AND Id > @postID
    ), 0);
END;

/* final day user calculations */
UPDATE fo
    SET
    fo.userMostResponses =
(

    SELECT ud.displayName
    FROM @usersDay ud
    WHERE ud.dayOfMonth = fo.dayOfMonth
                    AND ud.numPostsAnswered =
    (
        SELECT MAX(udm.numPostsAnswered)
        FROM @usersDay udm
        WHERE ud.dayOfMonth = fo.dayOfMonth
    )
)
, fo.percentagePosts = CASE
            WHEN fo.numPosts = 0
                THEN 0
        ELSE CAST(
(

    SELECT MAX(ud.numPostsAnswered)
    FROM @usersDay ud
    WHERE ud.dayOfMonth = fo.dayOfMonth
) / fo.numPosts AS DECIMAL(8, 7))
            END
    FROM #finalOutput fo;

SELECT *
FROM #finalOutput;
```

Functional Requirements

For each day in a given month, I need to know

- How many questions were posted?

- How many answers to those questions were posted, regardless of date?

- How many unique users answered those posts?

- What is the highest amount of distinct users that responded to a single question in that month?

- Which user responded to the most questions posted in that month?

- How many questions did that user respond to?

- What percentage of the overall questions posted in that month was that?

- How many of those responses were marked as accepted answers?

Data Calls

Table	Operation	Columns Returned	Filtering
dbo.posts	Select	MIN(Id)	CreationDate, PostTypeId
	Select	AnswerCount, AcceptedAnswerId, CreationDate	Id
	Select	MIN(OwnerUserId)	ParentId, PostTypeId
	Select	1	OwnerUserId, ParentId, Id
	Select	MAX(Score)	OwnerUserId, ParentId
	Select	MIN(Id)	CreationDate, PostTypeId, Id
	Select	MIN(OwnerUserId)	ParentId, PostTypeId, OwnerUserId

(continued)

Table	Operation	Columns Returned	Filtering
#finalOutput	Exists		dayOfMonth
	Insert or update	Row OR numPosts, numResponses	Single record (dayOfMonth)
	Update	numUsersResponded, numHighestUpvotesOneAnswer	Single record (dayOfMonth)
	Update	highNumUsersSinglePost	Single record (dayOfMonth)
	Update	userMostResponses, percentagePosts	Single record (dayOfMonth)
	Select	*	
@usersDay	Exists		Single record (userID/ dayOfMonth)
	Insert or update	Row OR numPostsAnswered, numAcceptedAnsPosts	Single record (userID/ dayOfMonth)
	Select	displayName	dayOfMonth, numPostsAnswered
	Select	Max(numPostsAnswered)	dayOfMonth
	Select	Max(numPostsAnswered)	dayOfMonth
dbo.Users	Select	DisplayName	Single record (Id)

Coding (Anti) Patterns

Datatype Matching

Datatypes from all temporary tables, table variables, and parameters match the datatypes in corresponding fields in the database tables.

Subqueries

The only subqueries occur on the @usersDay calls looking for certain aggregates (last update to #finalOutput).

Calculations

Most of the calculations are very simple (adding one or an integer to a column or variable). There is one division calculation at the end, but there is a check to avoid a divide-by-zero error.

Temporary Tables and/or Table Variables

- #finalOutput temporary table, narrow max possible rows – 31

  - Inserts: One row at a time

  - Updates: One row at a time (except last update)

- @usersDay table variable, narrow possible rows – several thousand

  - Inserts: One row at a time

  - Updates: One row at a time

Loops/Cursors

- While loop through all question posts in a month (roughly 50k–150k)

- While loop for each user responding to a post (roughly two users)

CTEs

None used

Join Types

Standard join types used, correct join syntax used

LIKE, NOT LIKE, and NOT IN

None used

Sorting Operations

- MIN(Id) from Posts in a time frame

- MIN(OwnerUserId) from Posts based on a ParentId

Calls to Other User-Defined SQL Objects

Select statements to dbo.Posts

Native SQL Functions in WHERE Clauses

Both statements setting @postID – DATEADD/DATEDIFF functions

Indexes

Can't be determined at this time

PART II

Database Structure

CHAPTER 3

Database Tables

In the following chapters, we're going to look at some different database objects and identify some common anti-patterns with each. We discussed many anti-patterns that apply to code such as stored procedures, functions, views, or even ad hoc SQL statements. However, each object type can have it's own pitfalls.

In this chapter, we're going to take a closer look at tables. If every piece of code touching a certain table is slow, the table definition should be examined. What exactly are we looking for in that definition? The information in Chapter 2 didn't really cover tables, except to mention computed columns. Well, let's start there!

Computed Columns

Calculations can have some unintended effects if they haven't been coded carefully. Make sure that there aren't any computed columns in your table that include user-defined scalar functions. Such columns can cause queries not to run in parallel even if the columns aren't included in the query output. Sometimes clever (too clever?) DBAs add columns to tables that divide by zero to catch out naughty developers who use `SELECT *` in their queries. If anyone tries to run a `SELECT *` query against a table with a column definition that includes a calculation dividing a number by zero, the query will fail with an error message. This is a sneaky way to ensure better habits, but it's really more appropriate to educate the folks writing code than to put land mines in the database.

Denormalized Data

If you aren't familiar with normalization, you should probably spend a little time reading about it. To touch on the surface, normalization is a practice based on set of rules about how the data in a relational database should and shouldn't be ... well, related. Most

63

© Lisa Bohm 2020
L. Bohm, *Refactoring Legacy T-SQL for Improved Performance*, https://doi.org/10.1007/978-1-4842-5581-0_3

people recommend following up to third normal form (3NF). There are more levels of normalization beyond 3NF, but 3NF is the current standard acceptable level that most people recommend adhering to.

First normal form (1NF) states that there should only be one value in any given cell. One way in which this is violated frequently is the inclusion of a comma-separated list of values in a single cell. This also states that repeating groups of columns is not okay – for example, having a column for comment1, a column for comment2, and so on. Additionally, in terms of the rules for 1NF, any data value should only be stored in one place. Lastly, all rows in a table should be unique and have a primary key.

A primary key is a unique identifier for a record. It does NOT have to be a GUID datatype; instead, the value for each record has to be distinct. This can be a single column or a group of columns whose collective values will be a unique key. Multicolumn primary keys can be concerning, but we will discuss that later in this chapter.

Second normal form (2NF) can be a little more difficult to understand. Every non-key value in a record needs to depend fully on the key value. A slightly less formal way of saying this is to make sure all the data in your table directly relates to the key. For example, you want the ID of the user who made a post to be in the `Posts` table, but you don't need to store information specifically about the user in the `Posts` table; you want to store information just about the post. Instead, we should have a separate table with the user information (like nickname) and a user ID (in our database, `OwnerUserID`) in the `Posts` table which relates back to the `id` in the `Users` table. The `OwnerUserID` would be considered a foreign key, which points back to the primary key (or Id field) of the `Users` table. Correctly set-up foreign key constraints can increase performance of a database as well.

3NF is similar in that you need to move any fields in a table that don't depend directly on the key from that table. Say the user's favorite color was a column in the `Posts` table. The favorite color column should be moved to the `Users` table instead of leaving it in the `Posts` table. The color is not directly related to the post ID; it IS directly related to the user. Thus, it should be in a table that has a key related to the user.

We're going to make up a story about the `dbo.WidePosts` table. Let's say that it was the original table for the StackOverflow database, and it still may be used for legacy reporting. As the application grew, tables were added or changed. So what happened to this table?

If you go look at the definition (or the list of columns) for the `WidePosts` table, you'll see… well, for one, it's wide (it has lots of columns). And secondly, what is `commentid1`, and `commentid2,` and all these comment columns with numbers in the name? It looks like denormalization of comment information, and that's exactly what it is. One of the problems with this is that you can't have more than five comments per post, which is somewhat limiting. Also, it's hard to break out the different comments. This table definition fails the definitions of both first and second normal forms.

We also have information about the user in this `WidePosts` table, which causes the table to fail the definition of third normal form. I specifically created this table for demonstration purposes; it's not one of the standard tables in the StackOverflow database.

Datatypes and Field Size

Most of the columns in the `WidePosts` table are an integer datatype and as such have relatively low storage needs. However, there are a few date fields and several large nvarchar fields: five nvarchar(700) fields, one nvarchar(max) field, an nvarchar(2000) field, and a couple of smaller nvarchar fields. The combination of several columns with some large varchar or nvarchar columns can represent a pretty sizable amount of data per row. Remember in the last chapter we touched on memory grants in queries? Large memory grant requirements can be affected by database table column datatype and width choices and can bloat the amount of resources SQL Server thinks it needs to run your queries.

How many of these column sizes accurately reflect the data contained in the columns? Let's look more closely at the data values in the `WidePosts` table. The query in Listing 3-1 will find the maximum length of the values in each of several columns.

Listing 3-1. Query to find max data value length in several columns of the WidePosts table

```
SELECT MAX(LEN(AboutMe)) AS AbtMe
        , MAX(LEN(Body)) AS body
        , MAX(LEN(CommentText1)) AS CT1
        , MAX(LEN(CommentText2)) AS CT2
        , MAX(LEN(CommentText3)) AS CT3
        , MAX(LEN(CommentText4)) AS CT4
        , MAX(LEN(CommentText5)) AS CT5
        , MAX(LEN(Title)) AS Title
        , MAX(LEN(Tags)) AS Tags
        , MAX(LEN(WebsiteURL)) AS WebURL
FROM dbo.WidePosts;
```

Table 3-1. *Results from the query in Listing 3-1*

Field	AbtMe	body	CT1	CT2	CT3	CT4	CT5	Title	Tags	WebURL
Max actual value length	2000	34357	600	600	600	600	600	150	107	188
Column definition length	2000	MAX	700	700	700	700	700	250	150	200

The first row in Table 3-1 shows the maximum length of the data values in the column specified. The second row shows the defined maximum length for each column. It looks like this table's columns were appropriately sized for the data that was going to be stored in the columns.

Deprecated Datatypes

Older tables can have datatypes that aren't really valid anymore. For example, as of the writing of this book, the datatypes text, ntext, and image are deprecated. Microsoft's recommendation is to use varchar(max), nvarchar(max), and varbinary(max) datatypes instead.

How Much Data?

We should understand how much data any table we're examining actually contains. The number of records, as well as the size of actual data in the table, can make a very big difference in how we approach rewriting the table, or if we even need to bother. We can use a native SQL Server stored procedure to get this information. The call to the sp_spaceused stored procedure to review the amount of data in the WidePosts table is shown in Listing 3-2.

Listing 3-2. Example call to sp_spaceused to find the amount of data in the WidePosts table

```
EXEC sp_spaceused N'dbo.WidePosts';
GO
```

Table 3-2. *Results from the sp_spaceused stored procedure in Listing 3-2*

name	rows	reserved	data	index_size	unused
dbo.WidePosts	1090572	3336672 KB	3292984 KB	42032 KB	1656 KB
In GB	1.09	3.34	3.29	0.04	0.001

Table 3-2 shows the number of rows, as well as some data sizes, for the WidePosts table. A million rows isn't considered "big" in the wild, but that number of records might be a challenge for your specific server setup or database. You should have an idea of the relative sizes of your tables and the data within them. The understanding of the data and index sizes will help you when you're looking at code, making it easier to understand why some queries may be performing poorly.

Data Skew/Cardinality

Cardinality involves how much unique data is in each row. Knowing the distribution of values in a column will help you find suboptimal query code and determine quickly which indexes might be helpful. Listing 3-3 will help us look at the cardinality of a few columns from the WidePosts table.

Listing 3-3. Query to find cardinality of some columns in the WidePosts table

```
SELECT COUNT(DISTINCT ParentId) as numParentIDs
        , COUNT(DISTINCT [Views]) AS numViews
        , COUNT(DISTINCT PostID) AS numPostIDs
        , COUNT(DISTINCT AnswerCount) AS numAnswerCounts
FROM dbo.WidePosts;
```

Table 3-3. *Results of the query in Listing 3-3*

numParentIDs	numViews	numPostIDs	numAnswerCounts
279298	3756	1090572	108

Table 3-3 shows us that the cardinality in AnswerCounts is pretty low – there are not a lot of unique values. There are a lot of unique PostIDs though. You don't have to run this exercise for all columns on a table, but I'd keep an eye on the ones that are used most frequently in the application to have a good idea of the cardinality of that data.

Constraints

Many tables have constraints, and there are many different types of constraints. Hopefully all of your tables have a primary key and a clustered index. If they do not, please add them! If you run the command in Listing 3-4, you can see the constraints against a table, as well as all sorts of other information about a table.

Listing 3-4. Example call to sp_help for information on the table WidePosts

```
sp_help wideposts
```

Table 3-4. *Last result set from the stored procedure call in Listing 3-4(some columns omitted)*

constraint_type	constraint_name	Status_enabled	Status_for_replication	Constraint_keys
FOREIGN KEY	Fk_WidePosts_PostID	Enabled	Is_For_Replication	PostID REFERENCES StackOverflowForBook.dbo.Posts (Id)
PRIMARY KEY (clustered)	PK_WidePosts_WideId	(n/a)	(n/a)	WideId

As we see in Table 3-4, the last result set returned from the sp_help command lists any table constraints that have been defined. Here we see the primary key and foreign key constraints on the WidePosts table.

Changing Table Definitions

Table changes can be tricky in how much they affect other database objects or the application. There are certain changes that are safer than others, and sometimes ways to mitigate the safety concerns in those changes that are considered "unsafe." If you have a data access layer that you can modify, that is the best of all worlds. By "having a data access layer", I mean that every call to the database goes through an intermediate layer. That intermediate layer can consist of .NET objects, stored procedures, and many other types of code.

The benefit to a comprehensive data access layer is that you can make underlying structural changes and update the data access layer. You do not have to worry about the many times the data may be accessed by code, since any access goes through the data access layer. If you don't have a comprehensive data access layer, though, you do have to worry about making changes to the underlying data structure and how that will affect data calls from the application, especially if you don't have a developer assigned to you to work with on these performance issues.

The safest method of dealing with table changes is to replace the table with a view of the same name and change the underlying structure. This may seem kind of foolish – what's the point anyway if we're just replacing the table with a view that more or less has the same definition as the current table? As we find more and more data calls referring to the original wide table, we can modify them to point to the narrower or normalized tables.

What kinds of changes? Well, we can normalize the comment data and move it out of the table that defines post data. This will allow us to have more than five comments per post. We can also separate out the user data so we're not saving the same strings over and over (e.g., the wide "AboutMe" column). This has the added benefit of allowing us to remove the problematic trigger we dealt with in Chapter 1, as well!

By referring to smaller tables, we can leave out some of the "extra" tables (the ones we're not pulling any data from) in queries, which will help lower our memory grants for those queries. We can also be more effective with indexing as well.

Let's build a view to mimic the WidePosts table, calling data from smaller tables that already exist in the database. In the cases that you'll be dealing with, it is unlikely that small, normalized tables will already exist in your database. We only see this here because I specifically created the WidePosts table for this example. You will most likely have to break up the data in your larger table into smaller tables that you create while doing some interesting querying to assist in your data move.

Please note: I recommend creating the view under a different name to start (not the same name as the table) and waiting to drop the table so you can test the output of the view to see if it matches the table select. Listing 3-5 shows the create statement for such a view.

Listing 3-5. View create statement for the WidePostsView view

```
IF (NOT EXISTS (SELECT 1 FROM sys.views WHERE name = 'WidePostsView'))
BEGIN
    EXECUTE('CREATE VIEW WidePostsView as SELECT 1 as t');
END;
GO

ALTER VIEW WidePostsView AS
SELECT
 p.Id AS postID
, p.AcceptedAnswerId
, p.AnswerCount
, p.Body
, p.ClosedDate
, p.CommentCount
, p.CommunityOwnedDate
, p.CreationDate
, p.FavoriteCount
, p.LastActivityDate
, p.LastEditDate
, p.LastEditorDisplayName
, p.LastEditorUserId
, p.OwnerUserId
, p.ParentId
, p.PostTypeId
, p.Score
, p.Tags
, p.Title
, p.ViewCount
, u.AboutMe
, u.Age
, u.CreationDate AS UserCreationDate
```

70

```
, u.DisplayName
, u.DownVotes
, u.EmailHash
, u.LastAccessDate
, u.Location
, u.Reputation
, u.UpVotes
, u.Views
, u.WebsiteUrl
, u.AccountId
, c.CommentId1
, c.CommentCreationDate1
, c.CommentScore1
, c.CommentText1
, c.CommentUserId1
, c.CommentId2
, c.CommentCreationDate2
, c.CommentScore2
, c.CommentText2
, c.CommentUserId2
, c.CommentId3
, c.CommentCreationDate3
, c.CommentScore3
, c.CommentText3
, c.CommentUserId3
, c.CommentId4
, c.CommentCreationDate4
, c.CommentScore4
, c.CommentText4
, c.CommentUserId4
, c.CommentId5
, c.CommentCreationDate5
, c.CommentScore5
, c.CommentText5
, c.CommentUserId5
```

```
FROM dbo.Posts p
INNER JOIN dbo.Users u ON p.OwnerUserId = u.Id
OUTER APPLY (SELECT coms.PostId
          , MAX(CASE WHEN theRowNum = 1 THEN coms.Id ELSE NULL END) AS
            CommentId1
          , MAX(CASE WHEN theRowNum = 1 THEN coms.CreationDate ELSE NULL
            END) AS CommentCreationDate1
          , MAX(CASE WHEN theRowNum = 1 THEN coms.Score ELSE NULL END) AS
            CommentScore1
          , MAX(CASE WHEN theRowNum = 1 THEN coms.[Text] ELSE NULL END)
            AS CommentText1
          , MAX(CASE WHEN theRowNum = 1 THEN coms.UserId ELSE NULL END)
            AS CommentUserID1
          , MAX(CASE WHEN theRowNum = 2 THEN coms.Id ELSE NULL END) AS
            CommentId2
          , MAX(CASE WHEN theRowNum = 2 THEN coms.CreationDate ELSE NULL
            END) AS CommentCreationDate2
          , MAX(CASE WHEN theRowNum = 2 THEN coms.Score ELSE NULL END) AS
            CommentScore2
          , MAX(CASE WHEN theRowNum = 2 THEN coms.[Text] ELSE NULL END)
            AS CommentText2
          , MAX(CASE WHEN theRowNum = 2 THEN coms.UserId ELSE NULL END)
            AS CommentUserID2
          , MAX(CASE WHEN theRowNum = 3 THEN coms.Id ELSE NULL END) AS
            CommentId3
          , MAX(CASE WHEN theRowNum = 3 THEN coms.CreationDate ELSE NULL
            END) AS CommentCreationDate3
          , MAX(CASE WHEN theRowNum = 3 THEN coms.Score ELSE NULL END) AS
            CommentScore3
          , MAX(CASE WHEN theRowNum = 3 THEN coms.[Text] ELSE NULL END)
            AS CommentText3
          , MAX(CASE WHEN theRowNum = 3 THEN coms.UserId ELSE NULL END)
            AS CommentUserID3
          , MAX(CASE WHEN theRowNum = 4 THEN coms.Id ELSE NULL END) AS
            CommentId4
```

```
            , MAX(CASE WHEN theRowNum = 4 THEN coms.CreationDate ELSE NULL
                END) AS CommentCreationDate4
            , MAX(CASE WHEN theRowNum = 4 THEN coms.Score ELSE NULL END) AS
                CommentScore4
            , MAX(CASE WHEN theRowNum = 4 THEN coms.[Text] ELSE NULL END)
                AS CommentText4
            , MAX(CASE WHEN theRowNum = 4 THEN coms.UserId ELSE NULL END)
                AS CommentUserID4
            , MAX(CASE WHEN theRowNum = 5 THEN coms.Id ELSE NULL END) AS
                CommentId5
            , MAX(CASE WHEN theRowNum = 5 THEN coms.CreationDate ELSE NULL
                END) AS CommentCreationDate5
            , MAX(CASE WHEN theRowNum = 5 THEN coms.Score ELSE NULL END) AS
                CommentScore5
            , MAX(CASE WHEN theRowNum = 5 THEN coms.[Text] ELSE NULL END)
                AS CommentText5
            , MAX(CASE WHEN theRowNum = 5 THEN coms.UserId ELSE NULL END)
                AS CommentUserID5
    FROM (SELECT Id
                , CreationDate
                , Score
                , [Text]
                , UserId
                , PostId
                , ROW_NUMBER() OVER (PARTITION BY PostId ORDER BY
                    CreationDate) AS theRowNum
            FROM dbo.Comments com
            WHERE com.PostId = p.Id) coms
    WHERE coms.theRowNum <= 5
    GROUP BY coms.PostId) c;
```

We can test the output of the view to see if it matches the table data using the code in Listing 3-6 (view data) to compare to the code in Listing 3-7 (table data).

Listing 3-6. Selecting top 100 records from the WidePostsView

```
SELECT TOP 100 postID
, AcceptedAnswerId
, AnswerCount
, Body
, ClosedDate
, CommentCount
, CommunityOwnedDate
, CreationDate
, FavoriteCount
, LastActivityDate
, LastEditDate
, LastEditorDisplayName
, LastEditorUserId
, OwnerUserId
, ParentId
, PostTypeId
, Score
, Tags
, Title
, ViewCount
, AboutMe
, Age
, UserCreationDate
, DisplayName
, DownVotes
, EmailHash
, LastAccessDate
, Location
, Reputation
, UpVotes
, Views
, WebsiteUrl
, AccountId
, CommentId1
```

```
, CommentCreationDate1
, CommentScore1
, CommentText1
, CommentUserId1
, CommentId2
, CommentCreationDate2
, CommentScore2
, CommentText2
, CommentUserId2
, CommentId3
, CommentCreationDate3
, CommentScore3
, CommentText3
, CommentUserId3
, CommentId4
, CommentCreationDate4
, CommentScore4
, CommentText4
, CommentUserId4
, CommentId5
, CommentCreationDate5
, CommentScore5
, CommentText5
, CommentUserId5

FROM WidePostsView
ORDER BY postID;
```

We need to compare the results of running the code in Listing 3-6 to the results of running the code in Listing 3-7, which selects the TOP 100 records from the WidePosts table.

Listing 3-7. Selecting top 100 records from the table WidePosts

```
SELECT TOP 100 postID
, AcceptedAnswerId
, AnswerCount
```

, Body
, ClosedDate
, CommentCount
, CommunityOwnedDate
, CreationDate
, FavoriteCount
, LastActivityDate
, LastEditDate
, LastEditorDisplayName
, LastEditorUserId
, OwnerUserId
, ParentId
, PostTypeId
, Score
, Tags
, Title
, ViewCount
, AboutMe
, Age
, UserCreationDate
, DisplayName
, DownVotes
, EmailHash
, LastAccessDate
, Location
, Reputation
, UpVotes
, Views
, WebsiteUrl
, AccountId
, CommentId1
, CommentCreationDate1
, CommentScore1
, CommentText1
, CommentUserId1

```
, CommentId2
, CommentCreationDate2
, CommentScore2
, CommentText2
, CommentUserId2
, CommentId3
, CommentCreationDate3
, CommentScore3
, CommentText3
, CommentUserId3
, CommentId4
, CommentCreationDate4
, CommentScore4
, CommentText4
, CommentUserId4
, CommentId5
, CommentCreationDate5
, CommentScore5
, CommentText5
, CommentUserId5

FROM WidePosts
ORDER BY PostID;
```

We should see identical results from the query in Listing 3-6 and the query in Listing 3-7. (Please note: The WidePosts table only contains the first 1,090,572 records from Posts and the other tables.) We can check the two result sets using a differential tool of some sort. I use Notepad++ which has a compare add-in, but there are many available tools out there for this.

Once we have verified that the output matches, we can drop the table and create the view with the name of the table. We should also drop the trigger on the Users table that updates the WidePosts table (we worked with it in Chapter 1), and we should clean up the test view we created in Listing 3-5. The cleanup code is in Listing 3-8, and the view create statement is in Listing 3-9.

Listing 3-8. Cleanup code for WidePosts table and associated objects

```
IF EXISTS (SELECT 1 FROM sys.tables WHERE name = 'WidePosts')
BEGIN
DROP TABLE WidePosts;
END;
GO

IF EXISTS
(
    SELECT 1
    FROM sys.triggers
    WHERE name = 'ut_Users_WidePosts'
)
DROP TRIGGER ut_Users_WidePosts;
GO

IF EXISTS (SELECT 1 FROM sys.views WHERE name = 'WidePostsView')
BEGIN
    DROP VIEW WidePostsView;
END;
GO
```

Listing 3-9. WidePosts view create statement

```
IF NOT EXISTS (SELECT 1 FROM sys.views WHERE name = 'WidePosts')
BEGIN
    EXECUTE('CREATE VIEW WidePosts as SELECT 1 as t');
END;
GO

ALTER VIEW WidePosts AS
SELECT
 p.Id AS postID
, p.AcceptedAnswerId
, p.AnswerCount
, p.Body
, p.ClosedDate
```

```
    , p.CommentCount
    , p.CommunityOwnedDate
    , p.CreationDate
    , p.FavoriteCount
    , p.LastActivityDate
    , p.LastEditDate
    , p.LastEditorDisplayName
    , p.LastEditorUserId
    , p.OwnerUserId
    , p.ParentId
    , p.PostTypeId
    , p.Score
    , p.Tags
    , p.Title
    , p.ViewCount
    , u.AboutMe
    , u.Age
    , u.CreationDate AS UserCreationDate
    , u.DisplayName
    , u.DownVotes
    , u.EmailHash
    , u.LastAccessDate
    , u.Location
    , u.Reputation
    , u.UpVotes
    , u.Views
    , u.WebsiteUrl
    , u.AccountId
    , c.CommentId1
    , c.CommentCreationDate1
    , c.CommentScore1
    , c.CommentText1
    , c.CommentUserId1
    , c.CommentId2
    , c.CommentCreationDate2
```

```
,  c.CommentScore2
,  c.CommentText2
,  c.CommentUserId2
,  c.CommentId3
,  c.CommentCreationDate3
,  c.CommentScore3
,  c.CommentText3
,  c.CommentUserId3
,  c.CommentId4
,  c.CommentCreationDate4
,  c.CommentScore4
,  c.CommentText4
,  c.CommentUserId4
,  c.CommentId5
,  c.CommentCreationDate5
,  c.CommentScore5
,  c.CommentText5
,  c.CommentUserId5
FROM dbo.Posts p
INNER JOIN dbo.Users u ON p.ownerUserID = u.id
OUTER APPLY (SELECT coms.PostId
            , MAX(CASE WHEN theRowNum = 1 THEN coms.Id ELSE NULL END) AS
              CommentId1
            , MAX(CASE WHEN theRowNum = 1 THEN coms.CreationDate ELSE NULL
              END) AS CommentCreationDate1
            , MAX(CASE WHEN theRowNum = 1 THEN coms.Score ELSE NULL END) AS
              CommentScore1
            , MAX(CASE WHEN theRowNum = 1 THEN coms.[Text] ELSE NULL END)
              AS CommentText1
            , MAX(CASE WHEN theRowNum = 1 THEN coms.UserId ELSE NULL END)
              AS CommentUserID1
            , MAX(CASE WHEN theRowNum = 2 THEN coms.Id ELSE NULL END) AS
              CommentId2
            , MAX(CASE WHEN theRowNum = 2 THEN coms.CreationDate ELSE NULL
              END) AS CommentCreationDate2
```

```
, MAX(CASE WHEN theRowNum = 2 THEN coms.Score ELSE NULL END) AS
  CommentScore2
, MAX(CASE WHEN theRowNum = 2 THEN coms.[Text] ELSE NULL END)
  AS CommentText2
, MAX(CASE WHEN theRowNum = 2 THEN coms.UserId ELSE NULL END)
  AS CommentUserID2
, MAX(CASE WHEN theRowNum = 3 THEN coms.Id ELSE NULL END) AS
  CommentId3
, MAX(CASE WHEN theRowNum = 3 THEN coms.CreationDate ELSE NULL
  END) AS CommentCreationDate3
, MAX(CASE WHEN theRowNum = 3 THEN coms.Score ELSE NULL END) AS
  CommentScore3
, MAX(CASE WHEN theRowNum = 3 THEN coms.[Text] ELSE NULL END)
  AS CommentText3
, MAX(CASE WHEN theRowNum = 3 THEN coms.UserId ELSE NULL END)
  AS CommentUserID3
, MAX(CASE WHEN theRowNum = 4 THEN coms.Id ELSE NULL END) AS
  CommentId4
, MAX(CASE WHEN theRowNum = 4 THEN coms.CreationDate ELSE NULL
  END) AS CommentCreationDate4
, MAX(CASE WHEN theRowNum = 4 THEN coms.Score ELSE NULL END) AS
  CommentScore4
, MAX(CASE WHEN theRowNum = 4 THEN coms.[Text] ELSE NULL END)
  AS CommentText4
, MAX(CASE WHEN theRowNum = 4 THEN coms.UserId ELSE NULL END)
  AS CommentUserID4
, MAX(CASE WHEN theRowNum = 5 THEN coms.Id ELSE NULL END) AS
  CommentId5
, MAX(CASE WHEN theRowNum = 5 THEN coms.CreationDate ELSE NULL
  END) AS CommentCreationDate5
, MAX(CASE WHEN theRowNum = 5 THEN coms.Score ELSE NULL END) AS
  CommentScore5
, MAX(CASE WHEN theRowNum = 5 THEN coms.[Text] ELSE NULL END)
  AS CommentText5
```

```
                , MAX(CASE WHEN theRowNum = 5 THEN coms.UserId ELSE NULL END)
                  AS CommentUserID5

                    FROM (SELECT Id
                          , CreationDate
                          , Score
                          , [Text]
                          , UserId
                          , PostId
                          , ROW_NUMBER() OVER (PARTITION BY PostId ORDER BY
                            CreationDate) AS theRowNum
                    FROM dbo.comments com
                    WHERE com.PostId = p.Id) coms
            WHERE coms.theRowNum <= 5
            GROUP BY coms.PostId) c;
```

Summary

Now that the `WidePosts` table has been broken out into smaller tables and normalized, we can use those smaller tables whenever we run into poorly performing code referring to the `WidePosts` view, which was formerly a table. There is one major concern with this method, though. Inserts, updates, and particularly deletes to the former table, which is now a view, can fail if the insert or update changes values in more than one of the underlying tables at once.

The concern about inserts, updates, and deletes makes this a great solution for read-only tables, but a less desirable solution for transactional tables. One way to mitigate data changes in transactional tables covered by a view is to use INSTEAD OF triggers on the view. Please be careful with INSTEAD OF triggers, as they can get exceptionally messy. I'd recommend against these triggers. If you have the ability to handle data changes in the application, I would make those changes in the application.

CHAPTER 4

Database Views

A view is simply a saved select statement. It does have some limitations that can be hacked around, but with views, "just because you can doesn't mean you should." A view can be called just like a table, and a view can call other views. The limitations on views are as follows:

- The select statement has to be the first statement in a view definition with the exception of CTEs.

- You can't order data in a view definition unless you use a TOP statement or FOR XML (I've seen plenty of SELECT TOP 100% in my day).

- Views cannot have default column values or constraints.

- Views cannot call temporary tables.

There are many common bad habits that developers fall into when using views. Let's take a look at some of them, using the following example. You get one of those infamous calls from one of your users. "Hey, we're trying to run this query. All it's doing is getting the number of linked posts for each post in a month, and it's taking well over 5.5 hours. Can you find out what's going on?" The user promises to send you a query, and you see the code in Listing 4-1 when you open your email.

Listing 4-1. Find number of linked posts using the linked posts query

```
SELECT wp4.postID
     , wp4.creationDate
     , wp4.numLinkedPosts
FROM WidePostsPlusFour wp4
WHERE wp4.creationDate >='20120801'
     AND wp4.creationDate < '20120901';
```

83

© Lisa Bohm 2020

L. Bohm, *Refactoring Legacy T-SQL for Improved Performance*, https://doi.org/10.1007/978-1-4842-5581-0_4

The code in Listing 4-1 taking 5.5 hours to execute might be the most ridiculous thing you've ever heard. How can this simple query take that long? Hmm… that table name doesn't look familiar. Well, it turns out that it's not a table, it's a view. Fine, fine, well, what's the view definition? When we pull the alter view statement from SSMS, we see the code in Listing 4-2.

Listing 4-2. View definition for WidePostsPlusFour

```
ALTER VIEW WidePostsPlusFour AS
SELECT wp3.*
            , dbo.getnumLinkedPosts(wp3.postID) AS numLinkedPosts
FROM dbo.WidePostsPlusThree wp3
WHERE wp3.commentID IS NOT NULL;
```

That seems almost entirely harmless, except possibly for the function getNumLinkedPosts. And wait, is WidePostsPlusThree another view?

Nesting

Nesting is a big issue when layers of views call layers of other views. This practice of nesting generally results in many calls to the same tables and can also result in the optimizer not being able to generate a reasonable query plan. A few folks in the community have done some research on this; and, at least as of SQL Server 2014, the optimizer couldn't do much better than a "good enough" plan on any views nested too deeply (past five levels). So what exactly is causing the performance problem with the code in Listing 4-1? Well, there was the stored procedure sp_codeCallsCascade that we discussed in Chapter 2, which can find all SQL objects that a specified object calls. We can execute this as shown in Listing 4-3 to find any objects that our WidePostsPlusFour view calls.

Listing 4-3. Sample call for sp_codeCallsCascade

```
EXECUTE sp_codeCallsCascade @codename = 'WidePostsPlusFour',
 @rootSchema='dbo';
```

Table 4-1. *Results of sp_codeCallsCascade example in Listing 4-3*

thisObjName	thisObjType	callingCode	Level
WidePostsPlusFour	VIEW	root	0
WidePostsPlusThree	VIEW	WidePostsPlusFour	1
WidePostsPlusTwo	VIEW	WidePostsPlusThree	2
WidePostsPlusOne	VIEW	WidePostsPlusTwo	3
WidePostsCh4	VIEW	WidePostsPlusOne	4
getnumLinkedPosts	SQL_SCALAR_FUNCTION	WidePostsPlusFour	1

As we see in Table 4-1, the WidePostsPlusFour view contains five nested levels of views! It also contains the scalar function getnumLinkedPosts. So, the question then becomes, what do the rest of these views look like? Even though the view WidePostsPlusFour looks like only a small amount of code, what really runs when you call it is the entire view cascade! So, for example, this view call would really look like the code in Listing 4-4 to SQL Server (and the Query Optimizer, which as you can imagine might be a little confused!).

Listing 4-4. Expanded code for WidePostsPlusFour, containing nested view code

```
SELECT wp4.postID
, wp4.creationDate
, wp4.numLinkedPosts
FROM (SELECT wp3.*
            , dbo.getnumLinkedPosts(wp3.postID) AS numLinkedPosts
FROM (SELECT wp2.postID
, wp2.AcceptedAnswerId
, wp2.AnswerCount
, wp2.Body
, wp2.ClosedDate
, wp2.CommentCount
, wp2.CommunityOwnedDate
, wp2.CreationDate
, wp2.FavoriteCount
, wp2.LastActivityDate
```

```
, wp2.LastEditDate
, wp2.LastEditorDisplayName
, wp2.LastEditorUserId
, wp2.OwnerUserId
, wp2.ParentId
, wp2.PostTypeId
, wp2.Score
, wp2.Tags
, wp2.Title
, wp2.ViewCount
, wp2.AboutMe
, wp2.Age
, wp2.UserCreationDate
, wp2.DisplayName
, wp2.DownVotes
, wp2.EmailHash
, wp2.LastAccessDate
, wp2.[Location]
, wp2.Reputation
, wp2.UpVotes
, wp2.[Views]
, wp2.WebsiteUrl
, wp2.AccountId
, wp2.PostType
, wp2.voteType
, wp2.numVotes
, commentUnpivot.commentID
, commentUnpivot.commentCreationDate
, commentUnpivot.commentScore
, commentUnpivot.commentText
, commentUnpivot.commentUserID

FROM (SELECT wp1.postID
, wp1.AcceptedAnswerId
, wp1.AnswerCount
, wp1.Body
```

```
, wp1.ClosedDate
, wp1.CommentCount
, wp1.CommunityOwnedDate
, wp1.CreationDate
, wp1.FavoriteCount
, wp1.LastActivityDate
, wp1.LastEditDate
, wp1.LastEditorDisplayName
, wp1.LastEditorUserId
, wp1.OwnerUserId
, wp1.ParentId
, wp1.PostTypeId
, wp1.Score
, wp1.Tags
, wp1.Title
, wp1.ViewCount
, wp1.AboutMe
, wp1.Age
, wp1.UserCreationDate
, wp1.DisplayName
, wp1.DownVotes
, wp1.EmailHash
, wp1.LastAccessDate
, wp1.[Location]
, wp1.Reputation
, wp1.UpVotes
, wp1.[Views]
, wp1.WebsiteUrl
, wp1.AccountId
, wp1.CommentId1
, wp1.CommentCreationDate1
, wp1.CommentScore1
, wp1.CommentText1
, wp1.CommentUserId1
, wp1.CommentId2
```

```
, wp1.CommentCreationDate2
, wp1.CommentScore2
, wp1.CommentText2
, wp1.CommentUserId2
, wp1.CommentId3
, wp1.CommentCreationDate3
, wp1.CommentScore3
, wp1.CommentText3
, wp1.CommentUserId3
, wp1.CommentId4
, wp1.CommentCreationDate4
, wp1.CommentScore4
, wp1.CommentText4
, wp1.CommentUserId4
, wp1.CommentId5
, wp1.CommentCreationDate5
, wp1.CommentScore5
, wp1.CommentText5
, wp1.CommentUserId5
, wp1.PostType
, vty.[name] AS VoteType
, COUNT(wp1.voteUser) AS numVotes
FROM (SELECT wp.*
      , pt.Type AS PostType
      , vt.Userid AS voteUser
FROM (SELECT
 p.Id AS postID
, p.AcceptedAnswerId
, p.AnswerCount
, p.Body
, p.ClosedDate
, p.CommentCount
, p.CommunityOwnedDate
, p.CreationDate
, p.FavoriteCount
```

```
    , p.LastActivityDate
    , p.LastEditDate
    , p.LastEditorDisplayName
    , p.LastEditorUserId
    , p.OwnerUserId
    , p.ParentId
    , p.PostTypeId
    , p.Score
    , p.Tags
    , p.Title
    , p.ViewCount
    , u.AboutMe
    , u.Age
    , u.CreationDate AS UserCreationDate
    , u.DisplayName
    , u.DownVotes
    , u.EmailHash
    , u.LastAccessDate
    , u.Location
    , u.Reputation
    , u.UpVotes
    , u.Views
    , u.WebsiteUrl
    , u.AccountId
    , c.CommentId1
    , c.CommentCreationDate1
    , c.CommentScore1
    , c.CommentText1
    , c.CommentUserId1
    , c.CommentId2
    , c.CommentCreationDate2
    , c.CommentScore2
    , c.CommentText2
    , c.CommentUserId2
    , c.CommentId3
```

```
, c.CommentCreationDate3
, c.CommentScore3
, c.CommentText3
, c.CommentUserId3
, c.CommentId4
, c.CommentCreationDate4
, c.CommentScore4
, c.CommentText4
, c.CommentUserId4
, c.CommentId5
, c.CommentCreationDate5
, c.CommentScore5
, c.CommentText5
, c.CommentUserId5
FROM dbo.Posts p
INNER JOIN dbo.Users u ON p.OwnerUserId = u.Id
OUTER APPLY (SELECT coms.PostId
            , MAX(CASE WHEN theRowNum = 1 THEN coms.Id ELSE NULL END) AS
              CommentId1
            , MAX(CASE WHEN theRowNum = 1 THEN coms.CreationDate ELSE NULL
              END) AS CommentCreationDate1
            , MAX(CASE WHEN theRowNum = 1 THEN coms.Score ELSE NULL END) AS
              CommentScore1
            , MAX(CASE WHEN theRowNum = 1 THEN coms.[Text] ELSE NULL END)
              AS CommentText1
            , MAX(CASE WHEN theRowNum = 1 THEN coms.UserId ELSE NULL END)
              AS CommentUserID1
            , MAX(CASE WHEN theRowNum = 2 THEN coms.Id ELSE NULL END) AS
              CommentId2
            , MAX(CASE WHEN theRowNum = 2 THEN coms.CreationDate ELSE NULL
              END) AS CommentCreationDate2
            , MAX(CASE WHEN theRowNum = 2 THEN coms.Score ELSE NULL END) AS
              CommentScore2
            , MAX(CASE WHEN theRowNum = 2 THEN coms.[Text] ELSE NULL END)
              AS CommentText2
```

```
, MAX(CASE WHEN theRowNum = 2 THEN coms.UserId ELSE NULL END)
  AS CommentUserID2
, MAX(CASE WHEN theRowNum = 3 THEN coms.Id ELSE NULL END) AS
  CommentId3
, MAX(CASE WHEN theRowNum = 3 THEN coms.CreationDate ELSE NULL
  END) AS CommentCreationDate3
, MAX(CASE WHEN theRowNum = 3 THEN coms.Score ELSE NULL END) AS
  CommentScore3
, MAX(CASE WHEN theRowNum = 3 THEN coms.[Text] ELSE NULL END)
  AS CommentText3
, MAX(CASE WHEN theRowNum = 3 THEN coms.UserId ELSE NULL END)
  AS CommentUserID3
, MAX(CASE WHEN theRowNum = 4 THEN coms.Id ELSE NULL END) AS
  CommentId4
, MAX(CASE WHEN theRowNum = 4 THEN coms.CreationDate ELSE NULL
  END) AS CommentCreationDate4
, MAX(CASE WHEN theRowNum = 4 THEN coms.Score ELSE NULL END) AS
  CommentScore4
, MAX(CASE WHEN theRowNum = 4 THEN coms.[Text] ELSE NULL END)
  AS CommentText4
, MAX(CASE WHEN theRowNum = 4 THEN coms.UserId ELSE NULL END)
  AS CommentUserID4
, MAX(CASE WHEN theRowNum = 5 THEN coms.Id ELSE NULL END) AS
  CommentId5
, MAX(CASE WHEN theRowNum = 5 THEN coms.CreationDate ELSE NULL
  END) AS CommentCreationDate5
, MAX(CASE WHEN theRowNum = 5 THEN coms.Score ELSE NULL END) AS
  CommentScore5
, MAX(CASE WHEN theRowNum = 5 THEN coms.[Text] ELSE NULL END)
  AS CommentText5
, MAX(CASE WHEN theRowNum = 5 THEN coms.UserId ELSE NULL END)
  AS CommentUserID5

    FROM (SELECT Id
            , CreationDate
            , Score
```

```
                            , [Text]
                            , UserId
                            , PostId
                            , ROW_NUMBER() OVER (PARTITION BY PostId ORDER BY
                              CreationDate) AS theRowNum
                    FROM dbo.comments com
                    WHERE com.postID = p.Id) coms
            WHERE coms.theRowNum <= 5
            GROUP BY coms.PostId) c
) wp   --WidePostsCh4
        INNER JOIN dbo.PostTypes pt ON wp.PostTypeID = pt.Id
INNER JOIN dbo.Votes vt ON vt.PostId = wp.PostID) wp1
INNER JOIN dbo.Votes vt ON vt.PostId = wp1.PostID
INNER JOIN dbo.VoteTypes vty ON vt.VoteTypeId = vty.Id
WHERE wp1.voteUser = vt.UserId
GROUP BY  wp1.postID
, wp1.AcceptedAnswerId
, wp1.AnswerCount
, wp1.Body
, wp1.ClosedDate
, wp1.CommentCount
, wp1.CommunityOwnedDate
, wp1.CreationDate
, wp1.FavoriteCount
, wp1.LastActivityDate
, wp1.LastEditDate
, wp1.LastEditorDisplayName
, wp1.LastEditorUserId
, wp1.OwnerUserId
, wp1.ParentId
, wp1.PostTypeId
, wp1.Score
, wp1.Tags
, wp1.Title
, wp1.ViewCount
```

```
    , wp1.AboutMe
    , wp1.Age
    , wp1.UserCreationDate
    , wp1.DisplayName
    , wp1.DownVotes
    , wp1.EmailHash
    , wp1.LastAccessDate
    , wp1.[Location]
    , wp1.Reputation
    , wp1.UpVotes
    , wp1.[Views]
    , wp1.WebsiteUrl
    , wp1.AccountId
    , wp1.CommentId1
    , wp1.CommentCreationDate1
    , wp1.CommentScore1
    , wp1.CommentText1
    , wp1.CommentUserId1
    , wp1.CommentId2
    , wp1.CommentCreationDate2
    , wp1.CommentScore2
    , wp1.CommentText2
    , wp1.CommentUserId2
    , wp1.CommentId3
    , wp1.CommentCreationDate3
    , wp1.CommentScore3
    , wp1.CommentText3
    , wp1.CommentUserId3
    , wp1.CommentId4
    , wp1.CommentCreationDate4
    , wp1.CommentScore4
    , wp1.CommentText4
    , wp1.CommentUserId4
    , wp1.CommentId5
    , wp1.CommentCreationDate5
```

```
, wp1.CommentScore5
, wp1.CommentText5
, wp1.CommentUserId5
, wp1.PostType
, vt.VoteTypeID
, vty.[Name]
) wp2 --WidePostsPlusTwo
INNER JOIN (SELECT CommentID1 AS commentID
            , CommentCreationDate1 AS commentCreationDate
            , CommentScore1 AS commentScore
            , CommentText1 AS commentText
            , CommentUserID1 AS commentUserID
            , PostID
        FROM dbo.WidePostsPlusTwo
        UNION ALL
        SELECT CommentID2
            , CommentCreationDate2
            , CommentScore2
            , CommentText2
            , CommentUserID2
            , PostID
        FROM  dbo.WidePostsPlusTwo
        UNION ALL
        SELECT CommentID3
            , CommentCreationDate3
            , CommentScore3
            , CommentText3
            , CommentUserID3
            , PostID
        FROM  dbo.WidePostsPlusTwo
        UNION ALL
        SELECT CommentID4
            , CommentCreationDate4
            , CommentScore4
            , CommentText4
```

```
          , CommentUserID4
          , PostID
     FROM   dbo.WidePostsPlusTwo
     UNION ALL
     SELECT CommentID5
          , CommentCreationDate5
          , CommentScore5
          , CommentText5
          , CommentUserID5
          , PostID
     FROM dbo.WidePostsPlusTwo) commentUnpivot
ON wp2.postID = commentUnpivot.postID
) wp3 --WidePostsPlusThree
WHERE wp3.commentID IS NOT NULL
)  wp4 --WidePostsPlusFour
WHERE wp4.creationDate >='20120801'
     AND wp4.creationDate < '20180901';
```

Wow, that's a lot of code! I didn't even paste in the definition for WidePostsPlusTwo for each of the UNION ALL statements, I just left the code calling the WidePostsPlusTwo view. Folks really need to understand what nesting views does in terms of the code, which is why the view code in Listing 4-4 is shown here. Although the definition for WidePostsPlusFour looks small in itself, when you dig a little deeper, you discover that it really is doing quite a bit of work.

Multiple Table Calls

When we have a big chunk of code, what's the first thing we need to do before we start trying to rewrite this? That's absolutely right – we document it! Let's start documenting the table calls, which we will show in Table 4-2. Instead of starting from the top down, let's start with the "insides" – that is, WidePostsPlusOne – and go "outward" from there.

Table 4-2. *Table calls from WidePostsPlusFour and its cascade*

Table	Operation	Columns Returned	Filtering
		WidePostsCh4:	
dbo.Posts	Select	A bunch	
dbo.Users	Select	A bunch	OwnerUserId (join)
dbo.Comments	Select	Pivot	
		WidePostsPlusOne:	
dbo.PostTypes	Select	Type	PostTypeId (join)
dbo.Votes	Select	UserID	PostId (join)
		WidePostsPlusTwo:	
dbo.Votes	Select	VotetypeID	PostId (join)
dbo.VoteTypes	Select	VoteType	VoteTypeId (join)
	Group By		
		WidePostsPlusThree:	
dbo.WidePostsPlusTwo	Select	A bunch	(x 6)
	Unpivot	Unpivoting comment info, for five rows per post	
		WidePostsPlusFour:	
dbo.WidePostsPlusThree	Select	A bunch	Where commentID IS NOT NULL
dbo.getnumLinkedPosts()	Function		PostId

A couple of things stand out in Table 4-2: the function and the multiple hits to the Votes table. Also, there's a pivot and an unpivot, which could be interesting in terms of performance. However, the table calls data is not enough for us to start jumping into a rewrite. Let's go look for some additional information.

Additional Pieces for Documentation

For each join in each of these views, do the datatypes match on both sides of the join? The answer here is yes, so we're going to avoid implicit conversion problems. There are no subqueries in any of these definitions besides the unpivot inner join subquery. There are some aggregates though, but nothing else that could remotely qualify as a calculation. It's a view, so we know there are no temporary tables or table variables. Likewise, there are no loops or cursors. Please note, however, that functions called by views can include temporary tables, table variables, loops, and/or cursors! Views do allow CTEs, but there are none of them here.

All of the join types we see in these views are quite standard, so no surprises there. In fact, the only other red flag item we find is the call to the function.

Know Your Data

Let's see how much data is "in" these views – or, as I should say, is called by these views. Let's do a simple count of the number of records in each view with the queries in Listing 4-5. We can also see what kind of time it takes these simple calls to run.

Listing 4-5. Queries to find number of rows called by the nested views

```
SELECT COUNT(1) FROM WidePostsCh4
WHERE postID < 1000000;

SELECT COUNT(1) FROM WidePostsPlusOne
WHERE postID < 1000000;

SELECT COUNT(1) FROM WidePostsPlusTwo
WHERE postID < 1000000;

SELECT COUNT(1) FROM WidePostsPlusThree
WHERE postID < 1000000;

SELECT COUNT(1) FROM WidePostsPlusFour
WHERE postID < 1000000;
```

The results of these queries are shown in Table 4-3. It is interesting to see how the number of records changes. The records decrease when there are GROUP BY clauses and increase when additional information that may cause duplication of records is joined to the dataset.

Table 4-3. *Number of records called by each view as determined by code in Listing 4-5*

View	Records
WidePosts	704,857
WidePostsPlusOne	5,677,176
WidePostsPlusTwo	85,922
WidePostsPlusThree	443,670
WidePostsPlusFour	70,635

When we run the STATISTICS IO and TIME output through the Statistics Parser web site, we get the data seen in Table 4-4. We see that these queries took… seven-and-a-half hours to run? Yipes! We also see a lot of read-ahead reads. What exactly ARE read-ahead reads?

Table 4-4. *Reads data from STATISTICS IO and TIME output from code in Listing 4-5*

Totals	Scan Count	Logical Reads	Physical Reads	Read-AheadReads
Comments	16,302,351	154,066,055	16,455,998	0
Posts	1	357,188,473	229,179	288,642,683
PostTypes	14	28	2	0
Users	2	137,315,320	345,900	6,661,228
Votes	27	6,579,846	262,615	6,516,446
VoteTypes	13	26	13	0
Workfile	1,134	2,640,232	313,074	2,347,454
Worktable	80,694,535	357,874,423	3,206,059	9,079,996
	CPU	**Elapsed**		
SQL Server parse and compile time:	0:00:10	0:00:13		
SQL Server Execution Times:	2:33:26	7:28:15		

When you ask SQL Server to return data, it's going to first look in the buffer cache to see if the data you need is there. If not, SQL Server is going to go get it from disk. According to Books Online (Microsoft's online documentation), read-ahead reads indicate the number of pages placed into the cache for the query. There is a lot of data being moved from disk into memory! IO caused by functions won't be included in the STATISTICS IO output, so there may be more reads that are happening when this code is run, attributed to the function.

Functionality Check

Let's go back and take another look at the original query, which is shown again in Listing 4-6. We want to take a step back and try to determine exactly what the query is trying to accomplish.

Listing 4-6. The original query we're examining

```
SELECT wp4.postID
      , wp4.creationDate
, wp4.numLinkedPosts
FROM WidePostsPlusFour wp4
WHERE wp4.creationDate >='20120801'
      AND wp4.creationDate < '20120901';
```

If we run the code in Listing 4-6 for a different time frame against the creation date – say from 20120801 to 20120802 – will it finish in a reasonable time? How about if we run the code for only an hour's worth of posts? Probably not – at least, it doesn't run in a reasonable time on my system. If you have the excellent hardware to make this work, then more power to you! (And I might be slightly jealous.)

We're asking for only three columns of data, but how much data are we really pulling with all of these views? What should we expect from a query like this? Let's pull the data directly from the Posts table, with the exception of the data for the number of linked posts. We'll do this using the code in Listing 4-7.

Listing 4-7. Pulling data directly from the Posts table

```
 SELECT p.Id
, p.CreationDate
FROM dbo.Posts p
WHERE p.CreationDate >= '20120801'
AND p.CreationDate < '20120901';
```

The code in Listing 4-4 returns 392,564 rows and has 16 ms of CPU time and 864 ms elapsed time. It scans the `Posts` table once and has 1074 logical reads. All we have left to do really to satisfy the functionality of the original query in Listing 4-8 is to add in the number of linked posts. Can we do this easily? Absolutely – it's a function! Let's add that in and try again with the code in Listing 4-8.

Listing 4-8. Adding a function to data pulled from the Posts table

```
SELECT p.Id
, p.CreationDate
, dbo.getnumLinkedPosts(p.ID) AS numLinkedPosts
FROM dbo.Posts p
WHERE p.CreationDate >= '20120801'
AND p.CreationDate < '20120901';
```

Wait! (And wait, and wait, and wait....) Yes, the code in Listing 4-8 took a while. In fact, I stopped it after 15 minutes. Why did it run for so long? Well, functions against a table field need to act once on each row. In this return set, we had 392,000 records return. That sounds like a lot of work to me! There are two ways to address this problem. We can change the function from a scalar function to a table-valued function, pass in the post ID set as a table-valued parameter, and get all the linked post data back in one set or rewrite the functionality of the function as part of the query. In general, I will always pick the second choice if the function is reasonable to rewrite. If it is 6000 lines or more, for example, I may rethink that choice. The function definition for `getNumLinkedPosts` is shown in Listing 4-9.

Listing 4-9. Definition for the getNumLinkedPosts function

```
ALTER FUNCTION dbo.getNumLinkedPosts (@postID int)
RETURNS int
```

```
AS
BEGIN
DECLARE @numPosts int;

SET @numPosts = COALESCE((SELECT COUNT(1)
            FROM dbo.PostLinks
            WHERE PostId = @postID),0);

RETURN @numPosts;

END;
GO
```

In the definition in Listing 4-9, we're getting an aggregate of data per post. How can we do that as part of a larger query? Well, we can use an OUTER APPLY to join to the main query. It has all the filtering benefits of a subquery (it only calls the data that's needed) but doesn't run row by row. We see what an OUTER APPLY would look like in Listing 4-10.

Listing 4-10. Replacing the getNumLinkedPosts function with an OUTER APPLY

```
SELECT p.Id
, p.CreationDate
, nlp.numLinkedPosts
FROM dbo.Posts p
OUTER APPLY (SELECT COUNT(1) AS numLinkedPosts
FROM dbo.PostLinks pl
WHERE pl.PostId = p.Id) nlp
WHERE p.CreationDate >= '20120801'
AND p.CreationDate < '20120901';
```

The code in Listing 4-10 returns 392,564 rows and has 8094 ms of CPU time and 8514 ms elapsed time. It scans the Posts table once and has 1074 logical reads and scans the PostLinks table once with 5824 reads. Additionally, we see a Worktable, which has one scan for each row and 5.3 million logical reads. What is that? Let's take a look at the execution plan, now that we actually have this code running fast enough to obtain one! The plan is shown in Figure 4-1.

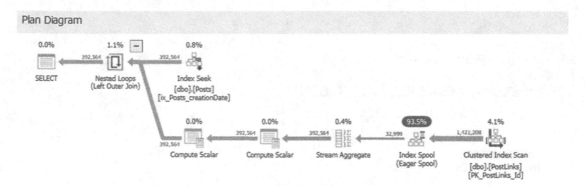

Figure 4-1. *Execution plan for the number of linked posts query*

As we look at the plan shown in Figure 4-1, we can see a clustered index scan on the PostLinks table and then an index spool which is where the vast majority of the work is happening. The index spool creates a temporary index on the predicates to join the data more efficiently. That's what an index spool is supposed to be doing, anyway. Here it appears to be a bit of a mess in terms of performance. Hmm, we are doing a count based on a PostId. If we added a nonclustered index on PostId, would that help? Let's try, using the code in Listing 4-11.

Listing 4-11. Creating an index on the PostID column in the PostLinks table

```
CREATE NONCLUSTERED INDEX ix_PostLinks_PostID ON dbo.PostLinks (PostId);
```

Once we create the index in Listing 4-11, we can run the query in Listing 4-10 again and grab the plan again as well. And, bingo! Even grabbing the plan, the query in Listing 4-10 took 3 seconds. To be precise, the execution showed an elapsed time of 3315 ms and only used 2765 ms of CPU time. The number of scans from the Worktable actually transfers to the PostLinks table, but in the STATISTICS IO output the term "scan" can actually refer to either a seek or a scan. The execution plan for the query in Listing 4-10 after adding the index in Listing 4-11 is shown in Figure 4-2.

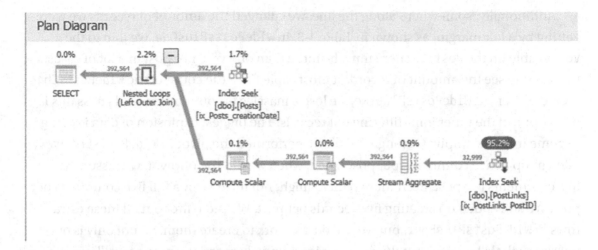

Figure 4-2. *Execution plan after index add*

As we look at Figure 4-2, we see exactly what we expect: the index seek is doing the bulk of the work. We have done well! We just took code that ran for hours on end, and now it runs in… 3 seconds. And to be honest, we didn't do that much work. In fact, we did a whole lot less work than what the call to the views did!

What Problems Did We Fix?

Why did this run so much faster than the original call to the view? Well, we showed how much code was really running in the background. It's easy to call a view, realize it has most of the fields that you need, and create a second view adding the one or two extra fields needed. The problem is that people keep doing that, adding more views on top of views, so the tables really are being called multiple times throughout the actual code being run. Since the view definitions can look deceptively simple, it's not obvious to the casual observer that all of the work underneath the view call is what is really happening.

Pivoting and unpivoting involve aggregates of some sort for each operation. The way I coded these views was (as of SQL Server 2014 at least) the same way the SQL Server engine handles them under the hood, even if you use the "official" pivot or unpivot syntax. Large GROUP BYs make SQL Server have to do the grouping specified, which almost always means a worktable. Then, it has to sort the data (there's no way to group data unless it's sorted to allow us to group, after all). Sorting is a fairly expensive operation in SQL Server. If there is already an index sorted in the desired order, it is possible to avoid a sorting operation, but if you create indexes to support any sort order on any column, then you run into the possible problem of having too many indexes which results in write times taking forever.

Additionally, somewhere along the line, we changed the amount of records we were getting by a fair margin, as shown in Table 4-3. In `WidePostsPlusOne`, we join to the `Votes` table on the `PostID`. There must be more than one vote per post in a lot of cases, because we see the amount of records almost triple from the count of the `WidePostsCh4` records. Then, in `WidePostsPlusTwo`, we lose a massive amount of rows. I'd guess this is due to one of the inner joins filtering out records. The biggest explosion of data is going to come from the unpivot, though. When we performed the pivot in `WidePostsCh4`, we filled in up to five comments per post. Then, when we did the unpivot, we "assumed" five comments per post, even though there might not have been a full five comments per post. We still ended up creating five records per post. We then filter out all these extra rows in `WidePostsPlusFour`, but we still do the work to create them. So not only is our rewrite a whole lot faster but the data in it is potentially more accurate as well!

Filtering

Filtering can be a challenge without reducing the usefulness of the view. You cannot pass parameters into a view. Your options then become hard-coding filters into the view if you want to limit the result set, or making sure every calling object contains a good WHERE clause. CTEs can be used in a view definition, which can be useful for filtering in certain situations.

Updating Data Through a View

This is easy in a single-table view. This is not easy (or, in most cases, not possible) in a multi-table view. Inserts and deletes will only work against a view containing fields from a single table. Updates can run against a view containing more than one table, but the updates must be against columns in a single table. These limitations exist because SQL Server's query engine can't always definitively trace a piece of data in a view back to the original table (can you imagine trying to run an update against `WidePostsPlusFour`?). If SQL Server can't trace the data back, it can't update data through the view.

Additional Limitations

You cannot create a view against a temporary table or a table variable. This makes sense if you think about it – the view definition is a permanent object in a database, whereas a temporary table, even a global one, is not, by definition: it's... well, temporary.

You cannot specify default values for columns, or constraints. You could use COALESCE, which would solve the default value issue (sort of), but there's no work-around for the constraints.

Why Use a View?

All of these limitations and performance problems sound really unfortunate. Why would anyone use a view if there are all these possible traps and caveats? Well, as we discussed in the previous chapter, we can start splitting up wide tables by creating a view to allow older calls to refer to the view instead and then start breaking up the tables so any code we modify or write in the future can point to the smaller and more normalized tables.

Additionally, views are really fantastic security tools. We can make sure that permissions to views are only given to the appropriate groups. For example, while HR might need to view social security numbers, no one else can or should be able to do so. If you have multiple divisions of a company, we can make sure each division uses their own view so they don't have access to the other divisions' data.

Summary

Hopefully you understand a bit more about the pitfalls that commonly surround views, especially the nesting problem. We also have learned that they can be useful for security purposes, or to help us break up wide tables into smaller, more normalized tables. Now it's time to look at some other types of database objects to find code we can fix to make our application perform better!

PART III

CRUD Objects

CHAPTER 5

Triggers

Triggers are objects that run when data changes (or in some cases, schema changes). They can run against tables or views and can be, well, triggered by inserts, updates, or deletes. There are some caveats on using them against a view (besides my personal opinion, which is: please don't).

Each trigger has two tables that you can use to query data that has changed. There is an INSERTED table and a DELETED table. If you are firing a trigger on an INSERT, there will be records in the INSERTED table but none in the DELETED table. If you are firing a trigger on a DELETE, there will be records in the DELETED table but none in the INSERTED table. If you fire the trigger on an UPDATE statement, there will be a record in both the INSERTED and DELETED tables that will contain the same primary key value, so you can join these records together to find data that has changed.

View-Based Triggers

One caveat is that view-based triggers must be INSTEAD OF triggers, meaning that the action in the trigger will happen instead of the original action performed against the object (here, a view). For example, instead of allowing a delete to happen, the INSTEAD OF trigger will run some other code, and the initial delete will not happen unless it is coded in that INSTEAD OF trigger.

INSTEAD OF triggers are what we would use if we changed a table's structure and used a view overlaying them to handle the legacy code. You could still insert, update, and delete to the "view" by using the INSTEAD OF triggers to manipulate the data underneath, allowing legacy application code to work against the new schema.

© Lisa Bohm 2020

L. Bohm, *Refactoring Legacy T-SQL for Improved Performance*, https://doi.org/10.1007/978-1-4842-5581-0_5

When Should We Use Triggers?

Triggers seem like a simple way of performing business logic, but this easy answer can spiral out of control very quickly. I haven't found many good use cases for triggers; the one that I have found is to use a temporary diagnostic trigger. We can use diagnostic triggers to track down a culprit who is making changes in data that are difficult to track. I'm sure there are a few others out there, but in almost all cases, the logic in triggers can be handled by a data access layer or the application in a way that will be less problematic than using the trigger.

Common Issues with Triggers

Trigger code can be very difficult to debug. It's easier for data integrity problems to creep in here because of this. This can happen in most types of objects, but I've seen integrity issues more commonly with triggers. Let's go back to our normal day, where we're having a lovely day at work. Then, we get a case ticket from user 1010297, saying that all their Reputation points disappeared, and they are pretty angry about this. What could have happened?

First of all, we'll need to look for the code that could have caused the change in the Reputation points. When we dig, we find that there is a trigger on the Users table. When we take a look at the trigger, it appears that the functionality entails a user who gains a multiple of 5 DownVotes. If their Reputation is greater than 0, they will get their Reputation reduced by 1. We have our trigger code shown in Listing 5-1.

Listing 5-1. The iu_Users_DownVotes trigger definition

```
IF NOT EXISTS (SELECT 1 FROM  sys.triggers
 WHERE name = 'iu_Users_DownVotes'
)
```

```
BEGIN
DECLARE @SQL nvarchar(1200);
SET @SQL = N'
/**************************************************************************
    2019.06.30    LBohm                    INITIAL TRIGGER STUB CREATE RELEASE
**************************************************************************/

CREATE TRIGGER dbo.iu_Users_DownVotes ON dbo.Users
FOR INSERT,UPDATE
AS
BEGIN
  SET NOCOUNT ON;
  IF NOT EXISTS (SELECT 1 FROM INSERTED)
    RETURN;

 END;';

EXECUTE SP_EXECUTESQL @SQL;
END;
GO
/**************************************************************************
  Object Description: Reduces User Reputation after 5 DownVotes.

  Revision History:
  Date            Name            Label/PTS    Description
  -----------     ---------------  ----------  -------------------------------
  2019.06.30      LBohm                         Initial Release
**************************************************************************/

ALTER TRIGGER [dbo].[iu_Users_DownVotes] ON [dbo].[Users]
FOR INSERT,UPDATE
AS
```

```
BEGIN
SET NOCOUNT ON;
-- if the DownVote count divided by 5 has no remainder, subtract 1 from the
Reputation
IF EXISTS (SELECT 1 FROM INSERTED i WHERE i.DownVotes > 0
      AND i.DownVotes % 5 = 0
      AND i.Reputation > 0)
BEGIN
UPDATE u
SET u.Reputation = u.Reputation - 1
FROM dbo.Users u
INNER JOIN INSERTED i ON u.Id = i.Id
WHERE i.Reputation > 0;

END;
INSERT INTO dbo.Triggerlog (id, thisDate, thisAction, descript)
SELECT u.Id, getdate(), 'Update', 'Update Reputation User table'
FROM dbo.Users u
INNER JOIN INSERTED i ON u.Id = i.Id
WHERE i.Reputation > 0;
END;
GO
```

Let's test with user 763725, who has a Reputation value of 1 and 4 DownVotes. An additional DownVote should put this user at 5 DownVotes and lower their Reputation to 0. We'll use the code in Listing 5-2 to test what happens when we add a DownVote to the user.

Listing 5-2. Adding a DownVote to user 763725

```
DECLARE @userID int = 763725;

SELECT Id, Reputation, DownVotes
FROM dbo.Users
WHERE Id = @userID;

UPDATE dbo.Users
SET DownVotes = DownVotes + 1
```

```
WHERE Id = @userID;

SELECT Id, Reputation, DownVotes
FROM dbo.Users
WHERE Id = @userID;
```

The first set of results, shown in Table 5-1, show the "before" state of the user. We see that the user's Reputation is 1 and they have 4 DownVotes. We can then see the results of the same select statement, run after the addition of a DownVote, in Table 5-2.

Table 5-1. *User 763725's Reputation and DownVotes score before an update*

Id	Reputation	DownVotes
763725	1	4

Table 5-2. *User 763725's Reputation and DownVotes score after adding a DownVote*

Id	Reputation	DownVotes
763725	0	5

Perfect! Table 5-2 shows exactly the results we wanted. The DownVotes increased to 5, and the Reputation decreased to 0. However, what we just tested isn't the only possible scenario. We just happen to have a working restore of production (in this case, our sample database), so we still have user 1010297's initial data. This will allow us to see exactly what is happening with this user! They have 14 DownVotes, so maybe someone added one, but that would have removed only 1 Reputation point, right? We will use the code in Listing 5-3 to test the scenario described by user 1010297.

Listing 5-3. Adding a DownVote to user 1010297

```
DECLARE @userID int = 1010297;

SELECT Id, Reputation, DownVotes
FROM dbo.Users
WHERE Id = @userID;

UPDATE dbo.Users
SET DownVotes = DownVotes + 1
WHERE Id = @userID;

SELECT Id, Reputation, DownVotes
FROM dbo.Users
WHERE Id = @userID;
```

We can see the "before" results in Table 5-3. The user had 14 DownVotes and a Reputation of 25. We can understand why they wouldn't want to lose all of those Reputation points! We can also see the "after" results in Table 5-4.

Table 5-3. *User 1010297's Reputation and DownVotes score before an update*

Id	Reputation	DownVotes
1010297	25	14

Table 5-4. *User 1010297's Reputation and DownVotes score after adding a DownVote*

Id	Reputation	DownVotes
1010297	0	15

Trigger Recursion

As we can see in Table 5-4, the user doesn't have any Reputation points left! Wait, where did all those Reputation points go? Well, let's look at the actual trigger logic again, shown in Listing 5-4.

Listing 5-4. Trigger logic for iu_Users_DownVotes

```
IF EXISTS (SELECT 1 FROM INSERTED i WHERE i.DownVotes > 0
      AND i.DownVotes % 5 = 0
      AND i.Reputation > 0)
BEGIN
UPDATE u
SET u.Reputation = u.Reputation - 1
FROM dbo.Users u
INNER JOIN INSERTED i ON u.Id = i.Id
WHERE i.Reputation > 0;
END;
```

What is the code in Listing 5-4 actually doing? It's updating the Users table. What fires this trigger? An UPDATE on the Users table. Hmmm... We are looking in the EXISTS statements for any record in INSERTED where DownVotes are greater than 0 and divisible by 5 and the Reputation is greater than 0. Then, we're reducing the Reputation by 1 for any record that meets the preceding criteria and is also found in INSERTED.

There are two problems here. One is that we're running an UPDATE that can fire the trigger itself again. The second problem is in the logic itself. In the preceding case, we're updating the table from 14 DownVotes to 15 DownVotes before we call the trigger. The trigger itself doesn't change the DownVotes value, so for the circumstance shown in Listing 5-3, the DownVotes value continues being divisible by 5, since that value will not change from 15.

This means that the Reputation will keep reducing by 1 for every run. We can also see that there were multiple runs of the trigger caused by the code in Listing 5-3 by querying the Triggerlog table (which is a table I set up specifically for this book). The Triggerlog table illustrates a point here but can be useful to add to any database that uses triggers regularly. The code to query the Triggerlog table is shown in Listing 5-5.

Listing 5-5. Querying the Triggerlog table

```
SELECT id, thisdate, thisaction, descript
FROM Triggerlog;
```

If we look at the results for the code in Listing 5-5, we can see the multiple firings for the user ID of 1010297. These results are shown in Table 5-5. The trigger code will actually fail after 32 recursions and throw an error message, if you try this update on a user with more than 32 Reputation points.

Table 5-5. *Results from querying the Triggerlog table*

id	thisDate	thisAction	descript
763725	8/21/19 15:03	Update	Update Reputation User table
1010297	8/21/19 15:05	Update	Update Reputation User table
1010297	8/21/19 15:05	Update	Update Reputation User table
1010297	8/21/19 15:05	Update	Update Reputation User table
1010297	8/21/19 15:05	Update	Update Reputation User table
1010297	8/21/19 15:05	Update	Update Reputation User table
1010297	8/21/19 15:05	Update	Update Reputation User table
1010297	8/21/19 15:05	Update	Update Reputation User table
1010297	8/21/19 15:05	Update	Update Reputation User table
1010297	8/21/19 15:05	Update	Update Reputation User table
1010297	8/21/19 15:05	Update	Update Reputation User table
1010297	8/21/19 15:05	Update	Update Reputation User table
1010297	8/21/19 15:05	Update	Update Reputation User table
1010297	8/21/19 15:05	Update	Update Reputation User table
1010297	8/21/19 15:05	Update	Update Reputation User table
1010297	8/21/19 15:05	Update	Update Reputation User table
1010297	8/21/19 15:05	Update	Update Reputation User table
1010297	8/21/19 15:05	Update	Update Reputation User table
1010297	8/21/19 15:05	Update	Update Reputation User table
1010297	8/21/19 15:05	Update	Update Reputation User table
1010297	8/21/19 15:05	Update	Update Reputation User table
1010297	8/21/19 15:05	Update	Update Reputation User table
1010297	8/21/19 15:05	Update	Update Reputation User table
1010297	8/21/19 15:05	Update	Update Reputation User table
1010297	8/21/19 15:05	Update	Update Reputation User table
1010297	8/21/19 15:05	Update	Update Reputation User table
1010297	8/21/19 15:05	Update	Update Reputation User table

We can see from Table 5-5 that the trigger fired many, many times. It fired once when we updated user 763725 in Listing 5-2, but 25 times when we updated user 1010297 in Listing 5-3. If we were still uncertain, we could change the INSERT to the `Triggerlog` table that is in the `iu_Users_DownVotes` trigger to include the Reputation points from the INSERTED table. You could then see the `Reputation` decreasing 1 point for each run.

Is there a way to stop the recursive trigger behavior? At the database level, there is a setting that allows triggers to fire recursively, which is turned off by default. There may be some situations in which people may want recursive triggers and turn the setting on. In this case, I have turned this setting to "on" (or 1, to be precise) for this database for these examples. You can check to see if the allow recursive triggers setting is on for your databases using the code in Listing 5-6.

Listing 5-6. Code to check if recursive triggers are allowed

```
SELECT database_id, name, is_recursive_triggers_on
FROM sys.databases;
```

If the setting is turned on, and we need to leave it turned on, we can still prevent recursion at the trigger level by using TRIGGER_NESTLEVEL(). We want to prevent calls to this trigger from this specific trigger. The syntax we want to add to the trigger is shown in Listing 5-7. There may be cases where we want to stop the trigger from being fired by any other trigger; in that case, you would use slightly different syntax.

Listing 5-7. Adding TRIGGER_NESTLEVEL() to prevent recursion

```
IF ((SELECT TRIGGER_NESTLEVEL(OBJECT_ID('iu_Users_
DownVotes'),'AFTER','DML')) > 1)
BEGIN
RETURN;
END;
```

We would want to add the code for the TRIGGER_NESTLEVEL() after the SET NOCOUNT ON; line and before the comment about the `DownVotes` count. We should test this, but first let's restore the poor user's Reputation using the code in Listing 5-8.

Listing 5-8. Restoring user 1010297's Reputation

```
DECLARE @userID int = 1010297;

UPDATE u
SET Reputation = 25
        , DownVotes = 14
FROM dbo.Users u
WHERE Id = @userID;
```

Once we've added the code in Listing 5-7 to our trigger and run the alter statement, we can run the test statements in Listing 5-3 again. The "before" results, shown in Table 5-6, are the same results as in Table 5-3.

Table 5-6. *User 1010297's Reputation and DownVotes score after restore and before an update*

Id	Reputation	DownVotes
1010297	25	14

The "after update" results, shown in Table 5-7, are much more what we had in mind. The DownVotes value is increased by 1, and the Reputation is only decreased by 1. This in itself shows that the TRIGGER_NESTLEVEL() was successful in removing recursion, but we should also look at our Triggerlog table. A check, using the code in Listing 5-5, will show you only a single record for the trigger at the time you ran the code in Listing 5-3 for the second time.

Table 5-7. *User 1010297's Reputation and DownVotes score after restore and after update to DownVotes*

Id	Reputation	DownVotes
1010297	24	15

Triggers and Multi-record Changes

There actually is another issue with this trigger. Have you realized what it might be? A lot of times, people assume that inserts and updates will occur only a single row at a time. This doesn't necessarily have to be the case. What if we are updating several users at once? Well, first go back, and let's restore user 1010297's Reputation with the code in Listing 5-8. Then, let's try running code in Listing 5-9 to look at multiple users at once. The results of the query are shown in Table 5-8.

Listing 5-9. Looking at DownVotes and Reputation for multiple users

```
DECLARE @theTable TABLE (id int);
INSERT INTO @theTable (id)
VALUES (1010297)
          , (1639596)
          , (2179513)
          , (2491405)
          , (2549795);

SELECT tb.id
          , u.Reputation
          , u.DownVotes
FROM @theTable tb
INNER JOIN dbo.Users u ON tb.id = u.Id;
```

Table 5-8. *Results of the query in Listing 5-9*

Id	Reputation	DownVotes
1010297	25	14
1639596	1	3
2179513	5	3
2491405	1	3
2549795	31	3

Table 5-8 shows us data for five users. If we incremented each person's DownVotes by 1, then the user with an Id of 1010297's Reputation should decrease by 1, but the others should not (they'd only have four DownVotes apiece). Let's take a look using the code in Listing 5-10.

Listing 5-10. Update DownVotes for multiple users

```
DECLARE @theTable TABLE (id int);
INSERT INTO @theTable (id)
VALUES (1010297)
          , (1639596)
          , (2179513)
          , (2491405)
          , (2549795);

SELECT tb.id
          , u.Reputation
          , u.DownVotes
FROM @theTable tb
INNER JOIN dbo.Users u ON tb.id = u.Id;

UPDATE u
SET DownVotes = u.DownVotes + 1
FROM dbo.Users u
INNER JOIN @theTable tb ON u.Id = tb.id;

SELECT tb.id
          , u.Reputation
          , u.DownVotes
FROM @theTable tb
INNER JOIN dbo.Users u ON tb.id = u.Id;
```

We saw the before results in Table 5-8. The after results are shown in Table 5-9.

Table 5-9. *Results of code from Listing 5-10*

Id	Reputation	DownVotes
1010297	24	15
1639596	0	4
2179513	4	4
2491405	0	4
2549795	30	4

Oh no! Each of these people had their Reputation decreased. When we look at the EXISTS statements in Listing 5-1, we're checking to see if a record exists where the DownVotes are divisible by 5. However, we do NOT check for the same criteria in the actual update statement! If we look in the Triggerlog table using the code in Listing 5-5, we'll also see a record for each of these users being run in the trigger.

If we modify the update statement in the trigger in Listing 5-1 using the code in Listing 5-11, we should only update the same records the EXISTS statement finds, and our results should be in much better shape.

Listing 5-11. New update statement testing if DownVotes is divisible by 5

```
UPDATE u
SET u.Reputation = u.Reputation - 1
FROM dbo.Users u
INNER JOIN INSERTED i ON u.Id = i.Id
WHERE i.Reputation > 0
        AND i.DownVotes > 0
        AND i.DownVotes % 5 = 0;
```

Before we modify the code in Listing 5-1 with the code in 5-11 and test, though, we should restore the users' Reputation points using the code in Listing 5-12.

Listing 5-12. Restore multiple users' Reputation points

```
DECLARE @theTable TABLE (id int, Reputation int, DownVotes int);
INSERT INTO @theTable (id, Reputation, DownVotes)
VALUES (1010297, 25, 14)
        , (1639596, 1, 3)
        , (2179513, 5, 3)
        , (2491405, 1, 3)
        , (2549795, 31, 3);

UPDATE u
SET Reputation = tb.Reputation
        , DownVotes = tb.DownVotes
FROM dbo.Users u
INNER JOIN @theTable tb ON u.Id = tb.id;
```

Next, we'll replace the UPDATE statement in the trigger in Listing 5-1 with the UPDATE statement in Listing 5-11 and run the alter statement. We will then rerun the code in Listing 5-10 to see what will happen when we update the DownVotes on these same five users. The before results should be the same as the initial before results, which were shown in Table 5-8. Our after results are different from before, and are shown in Table 5-10.

Table 5-10. *After results for updating multiple users' DownVotes at one time*

Id	Reputation	DownVotes
1010297	24	15
1639596	1	4
2179513	5	4
2491405	1	4
2549795	31	4

Whew! All better. Table 5-10 shows us that only the `Reputation` for user 1010297 decreased, which is what we wanted to happen. But is it really ALL better? Let's look at a scenario where we don't change the number of `DownVotes`. First please run the code in Listing 5-12 to reset our users' values back to starting values. The code for the lack of change for `DownVotes` values is shown in Listing 5-13.

Testing for Values Changing

Listing 5-13. Increasing the upvotes of four users

```
DECLARE @theTable TABLE (id int);
INSERT INTO @theTable (id)
VALUES (1010297)
     , (1639596)
     , (22)
     , (123);

SELECT tb.id
           , u.Reputation
           , u.DownVotes
           , u.UpVotes
FROM @theTable tb
INNER JOIN dbo.Users u ON tb.id = u.Id;

UPDATE u
SET UpVotes = u.UpVotes + 1
     , DownVotes = u.DownVotes
FROM dbo.Users u
INNER JOIN @theTable tb ON u.Id = tb.id;

SELECT tb.id
           , u.Reputation
           , u.DownVotes
           , u.UpVotes
FROM @theTable tb
INNER JOIN dbo.Users u ON tb.id = u.Id;
```

The results from the before query in Listing 5-13 are shown in Table 5-11. We see two users whose DownVotes are divisible by 5 and two users whose DownVotes are not equally divisible by 5. This shouldn't matter, though, because we're not changing the DownVotes anyway, correct? The after results are shown in Table 5-12.

Table 5-11. *The before results for code in Listing 5-13*

Id	Reputation	DownVotes	UpVotes
1010297	25	14	161
1639596	1	3	11
22	12816	5	202
123	29212	40	419

Table 5-12. *The after results for code in Listing 5-13*

id	Reputation	DownVotes	UpVotes
1010297	25	14	162
1639596	1	3	12
22	12815	5	203
123	29211	40	420

Table 5-12 shows us yet another problem! The last two records have had their Reputation reduced, but we didn't change the DownVotes. Were we checking to see if the DownVotes were changed? Well, no, we weren't. We were just checking to see if they were divisible by 5 and greater than zero. There's an UPDATE function for triggers that we can use to determine that, though, right? First, let's use the code in Listing 5-14 to restore user data.

Listing 5-14. Restore user data for four users

```
DECLARE @theTable TABLE (id int, upvotes int, Reputation int);
INSERT INTO @theTable (id, upvotes, Reputation)
VALUES (1010297, 161, 25)
```

```
        , (1639596,11,1)
        , (22,203,12815)
        , (123,420,29211);
UPDATE u
  SET u.Reputation = t.Reputation
      , u.UpVotes = t.upvotes
FROM dbo.Users u
INNER JOIN @theTable t ON u.Id = t.id;
```

We then want to add the UPDATE() function to check if the DownVotes were updated. That should solve the problem of a user's Reputation being decreased if the DownVotes were not updated, but just happen to be divisible by 5. We can see the syntax for the UPDATE function in Listing 5-15.

Listing 5-15. UPDATE function check to add to our trigger in Listing 5-1

```
IF EXISTS (SELECT 1 FROM INSERTED i WHERE i.DownVotes > 0
      AND i.DownVotes % 5 = 0
      AND i.Reputation > 0
      AND UPDATE(DownVotes))
BEGIN

UPDATE u
SET u.Reputation = u.Reputation - 1
FROM dbo.Users u
INNER JOIN INSERTED i ON u.Id = i.Id
WHERE i.Reputation > 0
            AND i.DownVotes > 0
      AND i.DownVotes % 5 = 0
      AND UPDATE(DownVotes);
```

Once we've put this code in the trigger from Listing 5-1, we can rerun the code from Listing 5-13. When we look at the results, we just got exactly the same thing, both for the before and the after SELECT statements! The after result set is the same as we see in Table 5-12, showing the last two users with a reduced Reputation again even though we added the UPDATE() statement. What is going on here?

Well, in our UPDATE statement, we technically updated the value although we didn't CHANGE the value. This is a huge "gotcha" that people miss all the time. If it actually matters whether the value changes or not (and I'd guess if you're putting it in a trigger, then it does), we need to test to see the value changes. We can accomplish this by checking if the INSERTED and DELETED values are different. But this is also an INSERT trigger as well as an UPDATE trigger, so there may not be a DELETED value for every record – that value may be NULL. How can we do this? We can actually do this quite elegantly, thanks to Itzik Ben-Gan who taught me the technique shown in Listing 5-16, which avoids a lot of case statements which are normally found in null handling, while still handling NULL being different than a stated value.

Listing 5-16. Testing to see if the INSERTED and DELETED values are different

```
IF EXISTS (SELECT 1 FROM INSERTED i WHERE i.DownVotes > 0
     AND i.DownVotes % 5 = 0
     AND i.Reputation > 0
     AND EXISTS (SELECT i.DownVotes EXCEPT SELECT d.DownVotes FROM DELETED
     d WHERE i.Id = d.Id) )
BEGIN

UPDATE u
SET u.Reputation = u.Reputation - 1
FROM dbo.Users u
INNER JOIN INSERTED i ON u.Id = i.Id
WHERE i.Reputation > 0
          AND i.DownVotes > 0
     AND i.DownVotes % 5 = 0
     AND EXISTS (SELECT i.DownVotes EXCEPT SELECT d.DownVotes FROM DELETED
     d WHERE i.Id = d.Id) ;
```

The code in Listing 5-16, when used in the trigger in Listing 5-1, will find all records that don't have a match in the DownVotes field between the INSERTED table and the DELETED table. It will not evaluate a NULL, but it handles the NULL in such a way that the NULL isn't considered part of the set that matches, so we get records for the inserted statements as well as the non-matching updated statements. We're not going to test this here, but if we inserted a user record with a multiple of 5 in DownVotes, this would reduce the Reputation by one on the INSERT. Let's set these folks' Reputation points back with the code in Listing 5-14 and then rerun the test from Listing 5-13.

The before results were the same as we saw in Table 5-11, but our after results look much better, with no modification to the Reputation, as shown in Table 5-13.

Table 5-13. *After results from modifying four users with the INSERTED/DELETED difference check*

Id	Reputation	DownVotes	upvotes
1010297	25	14	204
1639596	1	3	421
22	12816	5	163
123	29212	40	13

Our final revised trigger is shown here in Listing 5-17, with all of the changes we've made throughout this chapter.

Listing 5-17. Final revised iu_Users_DownVotes trigger

```
IF NOT EXISTS
(SELECT 1 FROM sys.triggers
 WHERE name = 'iu_Users_DownVotes'
)
BEGIN
DECLARE @SQL nvarchar(1200);
SET @SQL = N'
/********************************************************************
    2019.06.30    LBohm                    INITIAL TRIGGER STUB CREATE RELEASE
********************************************************************/
CREATE TRIGGER dbo.iu_Users_DownVotes ON dbo.Users
FOR INSERT,UPDATE
AS
```

```
BEGIN
  SET NOCOUNT ON;
  IF NOT EXISTS (SELECT 1 FROM INSERTED)
    RETURN;

 END;';

EXECUTE SP_EXECUTESQL @SQL;
END;
GO
/**************************************************************************

   Object Description: Reduces User Reputation after 5 DownVotes.

   Revision History:
   Date          Name              Label/PTS    Description
   -----------   ---------------   ----------   -------------------------------
   2019.06.30    LBohm                          Initial Release
   **********************************************************************/

ALTER TRIGGER [dbo].[iu_Users_DownVotes] ON [dbo].[Users]
FOR INSERT,UPDATE
AS
BEGIN
SET NOCOUNT ON;

IF ((SELECT TRIGGER_NESTLEVEL(OBJECT_ID('iu_Users_
DownVotes'),'AFTER','DML')) > 1)
BEGIN
RETURN;
END;

-- if the DownVote count divided by 5 has no remainder, subtract 1 from the
Reputation
IF EXISTS (SELECT 1 FROM INSERTED i WHERE i.DownVotes > 0           (
     AND i.DownVotes % 5 = 0
```

```
AND i.Reputation > 0
AND EXISTS (SELECT i.DownVotes EXCEPT SELECT d.DownVotes FROM DELETED
d WHERE i.Id = d.Id) )
BEGIN

UPDATE u
SET u.Reputation = u.Reputation - 1
FROM dbo.Users u
INNER JOIN INSERTED i ON u.Id = i.Id
WHERE i.Reputation > 0
      AND i.DownVotes > 0
      AND i.DownVotes % 5 = 0
      AND EXISTS (SELECT i.DownVotes EXCEPT
              SELECT d.DownVotes
                  FROM DELETED d
                  WHERE i.Id = d.Id) ;

INSERT INTO dbo.Triggerlog (id, thisDate, thisAction, descript)
SELECT i.Id
      , getdate()
      , 'User DownVote trigger ran'
      , 'DownVotes: ' + CAST(DownVotes as nvarchar(12)) + ';
          Reputation: ' + CAST(Reputation as nvarchar(12))
FROM INSERTED i
WHERE i.Reputation > 0;

END;

END;
GO
```

Limit the Work Your Database Must Do

You may ask why we have the IF EXISTS statement in the trigger, since we're only
running the update against the records we really want. An update can still fire, even if no
rows are updated. We want to minimize the amount of work our database does PERIOD,
so these kinds of checks are important.

Let's look at the LinkTypes table. It has two triggers on it that do pretty much nothing, and the names of those triggers are pretty clear about their function (or lack thereof). In the trigger shown in Listing 5-18, the INSERT trigger has an UPDATE statement that runs only on records WHERE 1 = 0.

Listing 5-18. Create statement for i_LinkTypes_doNothing

```
IF NOT EXISTS
(SELECT 1 FROM sys.triggers
 WHERE name = 'i_LinkTypes_doNothing'
)
BEGIN
DECLARE @SQL nvarchar(1200);
SET @SQL = N'
/********************************************************************
    2019.06.30   LBohm                     INITIAL TRIGGER STUB CREATE RELEASE
********************************************************************/

CREATE TRIGGER dbo.i_LinkTypes_doNothing ON dbo.LinkTypes
FOR INSERT
AS
BEGIN
  SET NOCOUNT ON;
  IF NOT EXISTS (SELECT 1 FROM INSERTED)
    RETURN;
  END;';

EXECUTE SP_EXECUTESQL @SQL;
END;
GO
```

```
/***********************************************************************
   Object Description: Doesn't do a thing.

   Revision History:
   Date          Name             Label/PTS    Description
   -----------   --------------   ----------   ------------------------------
   2019.06.30    LBohm                         Initial Release
***********************************************************************/
ALTER TRIGGER [dbo].[i_LinkTypes_doNothing] ON [dbo].[LinkTypes]
FOR INSERT
AS
BEGIN
SET NOCOUNT ON;

UPDATE lt
SET lt.[type] = lt.[Type]
FROM dbo.linkTypes lt
INNER JOIN INSERTED i ON lt.Id = i.Id
WHERE 1 = 0;

INSERT INTO dbo.Triggerlog (id, thisDate, thisAction, descript)
VALUES (0
, getdate()
, 'LT Insert Do Nothing Trigger Ran'
, ''
)

END;
GO
```

The only thing the trigger in Listing 5-18 will really do is insert a record in the Triggerlog table if it runs. Now, in order to prove that the UPDATE statement runs (even though there's no update actually done), we also have an UPDATE trigger that does nothing – well, except also put a record in the Triggerlog table. We can see the code for this trigger in Listing 5-19.

Listing 5-19. The create statement for the u_LinkTypes_doNothing trigger

```
IF NOT EXISTS (SELECT 1 FROM sys.triggers
 WHERE name = 'u_LinkTypes_doNothing'
)
BEGIN
DECLARE @SQL nvarchar(1200);
SET @SQL = N'/************************************************************
    2019.06.30    LBohm                    INITIAL TRIGGER STUB CREATE RELEASE
*************************************************************/

CREATE TRIGGER dbo.u_LinkTypes_doNothing ON dbo.LinkTypes
FOR UPDATE
AS
BEGIN
  SET NOCOUNT ON;
  IF NOT EXISTS (SELECT 1 FROM INSERTED)
    RETURN;

 END;';

EXECUTE SP_EXECUTESQL @SQL;
END;
GO
/************************************************************************
  Object Description: Doesn't do a thing.

  Revision History:
  Date            Name              Label/PTS    Description
  ----------      ----------------  ----------   -------------------------------
  2019.06.30      LBohm                          Initial Release
************************************************************************/
```

```
ALTER TRIGGER [dbo].[u_LinkTypes_doNothing] ON [dbo].[LinkTypes]
FOR UPDATE
AS
BEGIN
SET NOCOUNT ON;

INSERT INTO dbo.Triggerlog (id, thisDate, thisAction, descript)
VALUES (0
, getdate()
, 'LT Update do-nothing Trigger Ran'
, ''
)

END;
GO
```

Let's run a simple insert statement to the LinkTypes table, like the one shown in Listing 5-20. Then we will check the Triggerlog table using the code in Listing 5-5. When we do that, we see that the there are two records in the Triggerlog table, as shown in Table 5-14.

Listing 5-20. Simple insert to the LinkTypes table

```
INSERT INTO linkTypes (Type)
VALUES ('TTest');
```

Table 5-14. *Results in the Triggerlog table after insert to LinkTypes*

id	thisDate	thisAction	descript
0	2019-06-30 9:27:24	LT Update do-nothing Trigger Ran	
0	2019-06-30 9:27:24	LT Insert Do Nothing Trigger Ran	

There are a couple of things to note with the results in Table 5-14. The UPDATE trigger actually inserted the record BEFORE the INSERT trigger inserted its record. This is because the UPDATE statement ran within the INSERT trigger, so it (the INSERT trigger) hadn't completed yet when the UPDATE statement ran. All of the internal triggers caused by a call will finish before the external trigger causing the internal triggers to be called.

A diagram of the flow is shown in Figure 5-1. In our case with the code in Listing 5-20, the INSERT statement to the `Triggerlog` fired only after all the triggers (in this case one) from the UPDATE statement completed. Also, we did not actually update ANYTHING, yet the update statement ran and fired an UPDATE trigger.

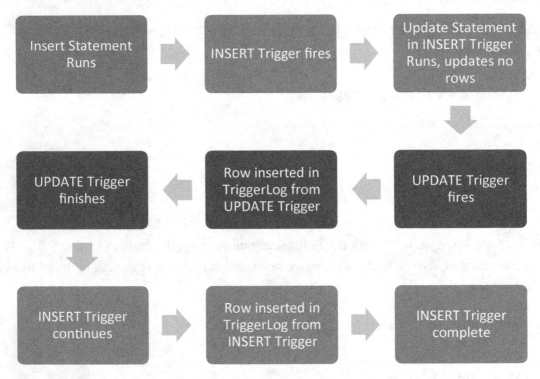

Figure 5-1. *Flow of triggers from insert on the LinkTypes table*

Imagine a vast, complex database with several triggers on each table. (I know, this sounds like a bad 1980s horror movie, but bear with me.) Any time you make changes to data in any table, there could be this really unpleasant cascade leading to a veritable trigger storm.

If we continue to spin this story out, we get to some triggers updating tables again, which can cause another round of update triggers to fire again... and again... and... Okay. I'm sure you can see where I'm going with this. You cannot specify which triggers fire in which order, either. For triggers against any table, you can specify a first trigger and a last trigger, but beyond that, you cannot determine the order in which they run.

In case that's not bad enough, if any of the code in any of the triggers fails, everything will then roll back. Not only do you have the performance hit of all these triggers running in the first place, you may then get stuck with the extra performance hit of all of them rolling back. This can make any save take a very, very long time.

Summary

One big lesson we learned in this chapter that doesn't directly relate to triggers is the importance of testing different scenarios. It's very easy and obvious to test that, in simple cases, the functionality you're coding works. It's less obvious to test all of the edge cases to make sure you aren't inadvertently introducing problems. Please make sure to write up your test cases thoroughly and make sure code passes all of these tests!

In terms of triggers, in almost every case, there is a way to accomplish the functionality you want without using a trigger. Their use introduces a potential for performance problems that can be difficult to find and troubleshoot. Just say no! Diagnostic triggers can be fine to use, but I would also hard-code a time limit on them so they won't fire after a month (or other reasonable time frame, depending on your application).

If you have a data access layer and denormalized tables, you can use your data access layer to propagate data changes to every table that needs those changes. Otherwise, business logic really should be handled by the application and not in the database.

If you are stuck with triggers, though, please make sure you check them all for the following:

1. They are only doing work when they actually need to.

2. They can correctly handle multiple records being updated, inserted, or deleted in the same statement.

3. Recursive firing has been handled correctly (be aware of your database-level settings and your trigger-level settings).

CHAPTER 6

Stored Procedures

In Chapter 2, we went ahead and documented a stored procedure used to call data
for a report. The proc was called dailySummaryReportByMonth. Let's review the
documentation from Chapter 2; then we can start to rewrite the stored procedure. When
we look at the data calls, we see six calls to the dbo.Posts table. There's a good chance
we can reduce the number of calls to that table. The proc also uses both a temporary
table and a table variable.

Temporary Tables vs. Table Variables

There is a lot of debate between whether to use table variables or temporary tables. There
can be issues with excessive recompiles of temporary tables inside of stored procedures,
leading to concerns. Most concerns were negated by better handling of temp tables in
later versions of SQL Server, but some still exist. For example, you should not change
the schema of the temporary table once it's created, even to add an index. Please add
indexes in line with the create statement. In this vein, temporary tables should not have
named constraints. There is a very good article by Paul White (https://sqlperformance.
com/2017/05/sql-performance/sql-server-temporary-object-caching) that
discusses issues around schema changes and named constraints at some length.

Additionally, be aware of adding or removing a large percentage of data from temp
tables; this should cause a recompile the way adding or removing large percentages of
data from regular tables will cause statistics updates and then recompiles of any procs
calling them. Here is a bit more information about recompiles: www.mssqltips.com/
sqlservertip/5308/understanding-sql-server-recompilations/.

Also, folks were saying for a while that temporary tables were stored in tempdb,
whereas table variables were not, but that really isn't true. Both structures will be stored
in memory until they are too large; then either can be written to disk. So what really
are the considerations of temporary tables vs. table variables? Well, table variables are

© Lisa Bohm 2020
L. Bohm, *Refactoring Legacy T-SQL for Improved Performance*, https://doi.org/10.1007/978-1-4842-5581-0_6

limited in the types of indexes that can be created against them. Additionally, temporary tables have statistics, and table variables do not. This can make a major difference in how they perform in terms of what kinds of execution plans get created. Because the optimizer cannot determine row estimates for table variables, I've found that it makes sense to use them only for very small tables (generally 100 rows or less, usually much lesser) where data isn't going to change much after insert. That is a personal choice, but I've found that it works pretty well as a general rule.

Please note that any time there is a "general rule," it means that there can be exceptions to those rules. In any recoding, it's always the best bet to try as many of the different permutations as you can, because there is no guarantee that a solution will really work best in each unique situation. If you've ever asked a DBA a question, please expect them to answer "It depends" because in almost all cases, it really does.

The Temporary Table

So let's talk a little about temporary tables. If there are going to be some joins against a key column, I'll generally set the temp table up to have that column as a primary key/clustered index combination when I define the table. I generally prefer not to add nonclustered indexes. If I can avoid that by writing more smaller pieces of code, or even procedures that do less work each, that is my preference, but sometimes that is not possible. When I come to code where the work can't be divided easily, I usually try rewrites of several permutations to find out which solution will work best in each case.

The Table Variable

Here, the @usersDay table variable will have one record for each user that responds to a post in a specific day. There are going to be many, many more records in this table than 100. This is an immediate flag that we'll need to change this to a temporary table – if we end up needing it at all. One good thing to know is how the rest of your application affects tempdb. Is the application a heavy user in general of tempdb, or is the use there light? If the code in your application already pounds on tempdb, you may want to be wary of adding more temporary structures that will increase the pressure on tempdb.

Loops

As we go through the documentation, we see two loops. The outer loop is handling each post during a certain day in a RBAR (row-by-agonizing-row) fashion. The inner loop is handling each user that responded to that post in a similar way. This is going to be the root of many, many of your problems. SQL Server is designed to handle data in batches or groups, not in a linear fashion, as we discussed in Chapter 2. Also as we discussed in Chapter 2, people think in a linear fashion. We accomplish one task (add a row to a table). We then perform another task (modify a value of that record).

Many front-end developers have a procedural way of thinking enforced because many applications work in that way also. Users view small groups of records, but usually interact with a single record at a time. Legacy code or code written by folks not as familiar with the SQL Server engine usually has a lot of cursors and loops in it. The best thing you can do for performance is to make them go far, far (FAR) away.

Because of the loops, it is extremely difficult to get performance data. There will be one section of output in STATISTICS IO and TIME for each time each loop runs. There will also be a separate execution plan for each query in each loop. This makes pinpointing a slow area difficult. With code like this, it's best to completely rewrite the stored procedure.

Functionality Review

What functions are being performed by this code? We're incrementing the number of posts for a day by 1. We're seeing if this user is the accepted answerer of a specific post. We're also incrementing the user count that touched the specific post by 1. We're grabbing the score for this specific user for this post and updating the temp table #finalOutput with some of that information. We're then adding a record into the @usersDay table if one doesn't exist, or updating the record if it does. And we're doing all of this for every single post. YUCK!

Start with the Simplest Data

When I rewrite code, I try to start with gathering the basic building blocks of data. This is the data I will need to get the desired output. I will start with the simplest data to query and then add onto the layers and complexity until I get the results that are needed.

For the dailySummaryReportByMonth stored procedure, what we actually need in terms of data is the following:

1. The number of posts in a day

2. The number of users that responded to any post that was entered in that day

3. The high number of users responding to a single post that was posted on that day

4. The user with the highest number of responses to a post on that day

5. The number of posts that a user responded to

6. The number of those answers marked as accepted answers

7. The highest number of upvotes for that day

So we have an initial select for every post created in the desired time frame, which is a question (PostTypeId = 1). We are going to limit our output for now to a small amount (a single day), which will make initial comparisons easier. We can use the code in Listing 6-1 to start replicating the stored procedure output.

Listing 6-1. Response posts for a single day

```
SELECT CAST(p.CreationDate AS DATE) AS createDate
     , p.Id
FROM dbo.Posts p
WHERE p.CreationDate >= '20120801'
     AND p.CreationDate < '20120802'
AND p.PostTypeId = 1;
```

The code in Listing 6-1 gives us 5,574 records, and we get our results in a relatively short return time. It's time to start adding more data to our response posts. Now we need to grab all the posts that are responses. These posts have the postTypeID of 2. We can add the answer count, the owner of the post, and whether this is the accepted answer. We can also add the score, which translates into upvotes. These additions are shown in the code in Listing 6-2, and a subset of results from the query is shown in Table 6-1.

Listing 6-2. Expanded data for response posts in a single day

```
SELECT CAST(p.CreationDate AS DATE) AS createDate
     , p.Id
     , p.AnswerCount
     , pUser.OwnerUserId
     , CASE WHEN pUser.Id = p.AcceptedAnswerId THEN 1 ELSE 0 END AS
       isAccepted
     , pUser.Score AS upvotes
FROM dbo.Posts p
     LEFT OUTER JOIN dbo.Posts pUser ON p.Id = pUser.ParentId
         AND pUser.PostTypeId = 2
WHERE p.CreationDate >= '20120801'
     AND p.CreationDate < '20120802'
     AND p.PostTypeId = 1
ORDER BY p.Id, pUser.OwnerUserId;
```

Table 6-1. First ten records from the result set for query in Listing 6-2

createDate	Id	Answer Count	Owner UserId	isAccepted	upvotes
2012-08-01	11750763	2	1530410	0	5
2012-08-01	11750765	1	868718	1	2
2012-08-01	11750767	1	841828	1	1
2012-08-01	11750768	3	8670	0	0
2012-08-01	11750768	3	814048	0	1
2012-08-01	11750768	3	1137672	0	1
2012-08-01	11750770	3	592212	0	0
2012-08-01	11750770	3	862594	1	3
2012-08-01	11750770	3	1567222	0	0
2012-08-01	11750780	1	1487063	1	1

Add More Data in Small, Easily Testable Increments

The results we see in Table 6-1 seem pretty straightforward and reasonable. Let's now look at adding some of the aggregates we need to mimic the functionality of the original stored procedure. We want to know, for a user, how many accepted answers they have. We'll use a case statement, and every time an answer is the accepted answer, we'll set the value to 1 and then sum those 1's. If the answer is not an accepted answer, we'll set the value to 0, so the sum will still reflect just the number of accepted answers. We also need the highest number of responses to a single post in a day, which we can get with a MAX() of the number of answers. We can use SUM() to tell us the number of answers in a single day. The query we use is shown in Listing 6-3.

Listing 6-3. Adding aggregates to our response posts for a single-day query

```
SELECT CAST(p.CreationDate AS DATE) AS createDate
     , COUNT(p.Id) as numPosts
     , SUM(p.AnswerCount) AS numResponses
     , MAX(p.AnswerCount) AS maxNumAnswers
     , pUser.OwnerUserId
     , SUM(CASE WHEN pUser.Id = p.AcceptedAnswerId THEN 1 ELSE 0 END) AS
        isAccepted
     , MAX(pUser.Score) AS upvotes
FROM dbo.Posts p
     LEFT OUTER JOIN dbo.Posts pUser ON p.Id = pUser.ParentId
          AND pUser.PostTypeId = 2
WHERE p.CreationDate >= '20120801'
     AND p.CreationDate < '20120802'
     AND p.PostTypeId = 1
GROUP BY CAST(p.CreationDate AS DATE), pUser.OwnerUserId
ORDER BY pUser.OwnerUserId;
```

We use a GROUP BY clause in Listing 6-3. The GROUP BY clause is going to aggregate the data per user. When we run the query, we get the result set shown in Table 6-2.

Table 6-2. *First ten records from running the query in Listing 6-3*

Create Date	Num Posts	Num Responses	maxNum Answers	Owner UserId	isAccepted	upvotes
2012-08-01	361	64	3	NULL	0	NULL
2012-08-01	66	187	7	0	22	62
2012-08-01	1	2	2	16	1	2
2012-08-01	1	2	2	95	0	0
2012-08-01	1	2	2	343	0	0
2012-08-01	3	7	3	476	1	4
2012-08-01	1	1	1	492	1	3
2012-08-01	2	3	2	536	2	11
2012-08-01	1	2	2	549	1	3
2012-08-01	1	3	3	631	1	0

Is the data in Table 6-2 the data we need for our query? Not exactly, but it is going to give us the building blocks we need to find the data we need. This query tells us

1. The number of distinct user IDs that responded to a post in this day (there is a record for each user ID)

2. Which user ID had the most answers

3. How many of those answers were "accepted"

It looks like there are some "default" OwnerUserIds that can probably be ignored. The values NULL and 0 seem to be "not real or valid" values, which we can check by seeing if there's a user id of 0 in the Users table. If we run the query in Listing 6-4, we'll see that there is no user in the Users table with an ID of 0.

Listing 6-4. Check existence of a user

```
SELECT * FROM users
WHERE Id = 0;
```

143

We should also discount these in the final query output. How do we get rid of these values? We want ALL ownerUserIDs except those that match the values of NULL or 0. This line will make that check for us and allow us to filter out those values. If you haven't played with EXCEPT or INTERSECT yet, I highly recommend doing so.

```
AND EXISTS (SELECT pUser.OwnerUserId EXCEPT (SELECT NULL UNION SELECT 0))
```

The next step in our rewrite is to remove these undesirable user IDs and then get aggregates over different groupings – some by post, some by day, and some by user. How do we do that?

Windowing Functions

What are those? Something installed on Windows? Well, I guess technically "yes," but in this case, they are functions included in later versions of SQL Server (some 2005 or later, others 2012 or later). What they do is take a "window" of your query results and allow you to do aggregates on them. Let's look at an example shown in Listing 6-5.

Listing 6-5. Adding windowing functions

```
SELECT p.Id
        , CAST(p.CreationDate AS DATE) AS createDate
        , p.AnswerCount
        , pUser.Score
        , COUNT(pUser.ParentId) OVER (PARTITION BY pUser.OwnerUserId) AS
          numPostsUser
        , COUNT(pUser.OwnerUserId) OVER (PARTITION BY pUser.ParentId) AS
          numUsersPost
        , pUser.ParentId
        , pUser.OwnerUserId
        , SUM(CASE WHEN pUser.Id = p.AcceptedAnswerId THEN 1 ELSE 0 END) OVER
          (PARTITION BY pUser.OwnerUserId) AS numAccepted
        , u.DisplayName
        , ROW_NUMBER() OVER (PARTITION BY pUser.OwnerUserId ORDER BY pUser.
          ParentId DESC) AS theUserRowNum
FROM dbo.Posts p
        LEFT OUTER JOIN dbo.Posts pUser ON p.Id = pUser.ParentId
```

```
        AND EXISTS (SELECT pUser.OwnerUserId EXCEPT (SELECT NULL UNION
        SELECT 0))
        AND pUser.PostTypeId = 2
    LEFT OUTER JOIN dbo.Users u ON pUser.OwnerUserId = u.Id
WHERE p.CreationDate >= '20120801'
    AND p.CreationDate < '20120802'
    AND p.PostTypeId = 1;
```

We can look at the result set shown in Table 6-3, which is a subset of the columns in our query in Listing 6-5, to see if we succeeded in getting the data needed. How did we get the number of posts each user responded to? We used a count of the post ID (it's the parent ID in the response link), and we partitioned by the user ID. We want to COUNT the pUser.ParentId, and we want the partition on this field defined by the pUser. OwnerUserId, so we use the following line:

```
COUNT(pUser.ParentId) OVER (PARTITION BY pUser.OwnerUserId) AS numPostsUser
```

Our "window" for the aggregate when we partition by the OwnerUserId is the set of posts a single user responded to, and the windowing function will return a separate aggregate for each user ID.

Table 6-3. *Subset of results from the query in Listing 6-4*

Id	Num Posts User	Num Users Post	ParentId	Owner UserId	Num Accepted
11766266	1	3	11766266	9465	0
11758727	3	1	11758727	9475	3
11756598	3	1	11756598	9475	3
11755899	3	1	11755899	9475	3
11766893	2	4	11766893	9530	2
11762529	2	3	11762529	9530	2
11759414	1	3	11759414	9686	1
11764539	1	17	11764539	9732	0
11755196	1	2	11755196	9922	1
11763636	1	2	11763636	10397	1

We're going to use the same "window," which is the set of posts a single user responded to in a day, for the number of accepted answers by the user ID. How can we do a sanity check, though? Run the query in Listing 6-2, adding an ORDER BY p.Id (the post ID). You can visually count how many different users responded to each post. Then run the code in Listing 6-5 again, also adding an ORDER BY p.Id. You can check the query without aggregates against the query with aggregates visually to see that the aggregates are correct for the entire query: you're getting the number of posts that user answered for every record that has that user on it. You'll see the same for the number of users that answered a post. Performing sanity checks like this often can help you from straying down the wrong programming path and save you time when troubleshooting!

Avoiding Row or Data Duplicates

Of course, we're getting potentially multiple records per post ID since we joined to the post responses, and there can be more than one response per post. We use ROW_NUMBER() in the query in Listing 6-5 to help deal with this issue. The ROW_NUMBER() allows you to assign a unique incrementing integer to a row based on the partitioning of your choice and also ordered by the values of your choice. This ROW_NUMBER() will help us filter out the "extra" rows (those rows which can lead to multiplying data and incorrect results).

We need the number of distinct users, so we can give those distinct users a row number as we did in Listing 6-5, and then just count the number of records where the ROW_NUMBER() equals 1. Wait, what? If we set up a ROW_NUMBER, partition by OwnerUserId, and order by just about anything, each new user will have one row (and only one row) with a ROW_NUMBER() equal to 1. So if we use a CASE statement and give each row that has theUserRowNum equal to 1 a value of "1" and all other rows a value of "0" and sum those values, we'll get a distinct count of users. Pretty cool, eh? This is also demonstrated in Listing 6-6.

Listing 6-6. Adding an outer query with some additional ROW_NUMBERs

```
SELECT theInfo.Id -- level two
        , theInfo.createDate
        , theInfo.AnswerCount
        , MAX(theInfo.Score) OVER () AS maxUpvotes
        , MAX(theInfo.numPostsUser) OVER () AS maxPostsUser
```

```
                    , theInfo.numPostsUser
                    , theInfo.DisplayName
                    , MAX(theInfo.numUsersPost) OVER () AS maxNumUsersPost
                    , theInfo.numAccepted
                    , SUM(CASE WHEN theInfo.theUserRowNum = 1 THEN 1 ELSE 0 END)
                      OVER () AS numDistinctUsers
                    , ROW_NUMBER() OVER (PARTITION BY ID ORDER BY numPostsUser
                      DESC) AS theIDRow
                  FROM (SELECT p.Id -- level one - innermost
                    , CAST(p.CreationDate AS DATE) AS createDate
                    , p.AnswerCount
                    , pUser.Score
                    , COUNT(pUser.ParentId) OVER (PARTITION BY pUser.OwnerUserId)
                      AS numPostsUser
                    , COUNT(pUser.OwnerUserId) OVER (PARTITION BY pUser.ParentId)
                      AS numUsersPost
                    , pUser.ParentId
                    , pUser.OwnerUserId
                    , SUM(CASE WHEN pUser.Id = p.AcceptedAnswerId THEN 1 ELSE 0
                      END) OVER (PARTITION BY pUser.OwnerUserId) AS numAccepted
                    , u.DisplayName
                    , ROW_NUMBER() OVER (PARTITION BY pUser.OwnerUserId ORDER BY
                      pUser.ParentId DESC) AS theUserRowNum
FROM dbo.Posts p
      LEFT OUTER JOIN dbo.Posts pUser ON p.Id = pUser.ParentId
            AND EXISTS (SELECT pUser.OwnerUserId EXCEPT (SELECT NULL UNION
            SELECT 0))
            AND pUser.PostTypeId = 2
      LEFT OUTER JOIN dbo.Users u ON pUser.OwnerUserId = u.Id
WHERE p.CreationDate >= '20120801'
      AND p.CreationDate < '20120802'
      AND p.PostTypeId = 1) theInfo;
```

The code in Listing 6-6 added a second level to the query. This outer wrapper is where we can perform additional aggregates, such as the CASE statement referring to the theUserRowNum which gives us the count of distinct users from our inner query. We also added a ROW_NUMBER in the outer query, but we'll talk a little bit more about why we did so a little later.

What exactly does this OVER() clause mean? It's a way to do the aggregate over a set. If there is no PARTITION specified, the data is aggregated over the entire query result set. This can be accomplished instead by using a GROUP BY clause, but we also need to see some detail rows; we're going to have to pull the correct user DisplayName for the user that had the most responses to each post so we can determine who had the most for any post during the day. If we use a GROUP BY clause, we'll lose the level of detail that corresponds with pulling all of these display names, as well as the number of posts per user. With windowing functions, we can get our overall aggregates without losing that detail. We're going to rely on the MAX() values whenever we can, because extra or duplicated rows won't affect those aggregates (extra rows will affect counts and sums but not MAX() and MIN() values). We can see some results for the query in Listing 6-6 in Table 6-4.

Table 6-4. *Subset of results from the code in Listing 6-6*

Id	Max Upvotes	Max Posts User	Display Name	Num Posts User	Num Accepted	Num Distinct Users	The ID Row
11750763	1,179	25	waldyr.ar	2	0	5506	1
11750765	1,179	25	Steve Koch	1	1	5506	1
11750767	1179	25	mwengler	2	2	5506	1
11750768	1,179	25	Annjawn	5	1	5506	1
11750768	1,179	25	Tom	2	1	5506	2
11750768	1179	25	DCookie	1	0	5506	3
11750770	1,179	25	nickb	11	8	5506	1
11750770	1,179	25	Miro Hudak	6	2	5506	2
11750770	1179	25	sriansri	1	0	5506	3
11750780	1179	25	Dustin	8	2	5506	1

The overall aggregates are going to show the same value in each row, as we see in the NumDistinctUsers, MaxPostsUser, and MaxUpvotes columns in Table 6-4. These columns are the building blocks to find the user whose number of responses is equivalent to the most responses. We can use that as a filter in... you guessed it, the next level (or level 3, which we will add). And we assigned a ROW_NUMBER() partitioned by post ID in level 2, so we can easily grab only a single row for each original post (this will make our COUNT() and SUM() data correct by excluding "extra" or multiplied rows due to joins). We can see that ROW_NUMBER() in level 2 in the code in Listing 6-6.

Listing 6-7 introduces us to the addition of a third level to the query. In this level, we will use the filter of theIDRow equaling 1. If you look at the code in Listing 6-6, you'll notice that we ordered theIDRow by numPostsUser DESC. Why did we choose that ORDER BY clause? Well, we also need to know the highest number of posts answered by a user, and this will give us this information. The ORDER BY using the by numPostsUser DESC means that the row with the highest value in the numPostsUser column will be given a ROW_NUMBER() equal to 1, which will give us the desired value for that field (numPostsUser) when we choose theIDRow equal to 1. And, if we group this by the creation date, we can then add more days and hopefully get the results we want! We'll try this a little later.

Listing 6-7. Query with filtering using aggregates and ROW_NUMBER()

```
SELECT COUNT(secInfo.Id) AS numPosts  -- level three - outermost
        , secInfo.createDate
        , SUM(secInfo.answerCount) AS numResponses
        , MAX(secInfo.maxUpvotes) AS numHighestUpvotesOneAnswer
        , MAX(secInfo.maxPostsUser) AS maxPostsuser
        , MAX(CASE WHEN secInfo.maxPostsUser = secInfo.numPostsUser
          THEN secInfo.DisplayName ELSE NULL END) AS userMostPosts
        , MAX(CASE WHEN secInfo.maxPostsUser = secInfo.numPostsUser
          THEN secInfo.numAccepted ELSE O END) AS numAccepted
        , MAX(secInfo.numDistinctUsers) AS numUsersResponded
FROM (
SELECT theInfo.Id -- level two
        , theInfo.createDate
        , theInfo.AnswerCount
        , MAX(theInfo.Score) OVER () AS maxUpvotes
        , MAX(theInfo.numPostsUser) OVER () AS maxPostsUser
        , theInfo.numPostsUser
        , theInfo.DisplayName
```

```
            , MAX(theInfo.numUsersPost) OVER () AS maxNumUsersPost
            , theInfo.numAccepted
            , SUM(CASE WHEN theInfo.theUserRowNum = 1 THEN 1 ELSE 0 END)
              OVER () AS numDistinctUsers
            , ROW_NUMBER() OVER (PARTITION BY Id ORDER BY numPostsUser
              DESC) AS theIDRow
FROM (
SELECT p.Id -- level one - innermost
            , CAST(p.CreationDate AS DATE) AS createDate
            , p.AnswerCount
            , pUser.Score
            , COUNT(pUser.ParentId) OVER (PARTITION BY pUser.OwnerUserId)
              AS numPostsUser
            , COUNT(pUser.OwnerUserId) OVER (PARTITION BY pUser.ParentId)
              AS numUsersPost
            , pUser.ParentId
            , pUser.OwnerUserId
            , SUM(CASE WHEN pUser.Id = p.AcceptedAnswerId THEN 1 ELSE 0
              END) OVER (PARTITION BY pUser.OwnerUserId) AS numAccepted
            , u.DisplayName
            , ROW_NUMBER() OVER (PARTITION BY pUser.OwnerUserId ORDER BY
              pUser.ParentId DESC) AS theUserRowNum
FROM dbo.Posts p
      LEFT OUTER JOIN dbo.Posts pUser ON p.Id = pUser.ParentId
            AND EXISTS (SELECT pUser.OwnerUserId EXCEPT (SELECT NULL UNION
            SELECT 0))
            AND pUser.PostTypeId = 2
      LEFT OUTER JOIN dbo.Users u ON pUser.OwnerUserId = u.Id
WHERE p.CreationDate >= '20120801'
      AND p.CreationDate < '20120802'
      AND p.PostTypeId = 1) theInfo

) secInfo
WHERE secInfo.theIDRow = 1
GROUP BY secInfo.createDate;
```

When we run the query in Listing 6-7, we get the single-row result shown in Table 6-5. It seems to contain most of the information we need for the report. Let's go ahead and take a line-by-line look at what we're getting from our query, though, because sanity checks are valuable.

Table 6-5. *Output from query in Listing 6-7*

Num Posts	Create Date	Num Responses	Num Highest Upvotes One Answer	Max Posts user	User Most Posts	Num Accepted	Num Users Responded
5574	2012-08-01	10,248	1,179	25	Jon Skeet	16	5506

How Did We Get Here Again?

Let's go back over the output statements from the code in Listing 6-7 and follow them through to see how we got to the final query.

```
COUNT(secInfo.Id) AS numPosts
```

The numPosts code line gets the number of posts for a day (well, in the code in Listing 6-7, we're just running the query for a single day). Also, in the outermost or third level, we're grouping by the createDate, which is the date with the time stripped out of the creationDate column. How are we avoiding duplicates of original post IDs, though? In the second level, we use ROW_NUMBER() partitioned by the ID. Then, in the third or outermost level of the query, we have in our WHERE clause:

```
WHERE secInfo.theIDRow = 1
```

This will only pull a single row per post ID, since we partitioned on the ID and there can only be one ROW_NUMBER() of 1 per ID.

```
, secInfo.createDate
```

The createDate is one of our simpler lines. We just cast the post creationDate to a DATE datatype, which strips out the time segment from the datetime. We can then group by that value, giving us information for a single day.

```
, SUM(secInfo.answerCount) AS numResponses
```

The numResponses is the sum of the answerCount, or the sum of the number of answers for each post in a day. We can do the sum on the third or outermost level, because on the third level we're only pulling one row per ID for that level and that row should always have the same number for the answerCount as any other row for that ID.

```
, MAX(secInfo.maxUpvotes) AS numHighestUpvotesOneAnswer
```

The numHighestUpvotesOneAnswer is a MAX() of a MAX(). Why is this? We want to group the outer query by the createDate, and we want all of the rest of the fields to be aggregates. In the second level, we're finding the maxUpvotes per ID. Then, in the outermost or third level, we need to find the MAX() of THOSE values, or the highest value overall in the maxUpvotes per ID.

```
, MAX(theInfo.numPostsUser) OVER () AS maxPostsUser
```

The maxPostsUser is a MAX() of a MAX() of a COUNT(). The COUNT() counts the number of times the user ID "owns" a post that has a ParentId (in our case, a response). We need the COUNT() to determine the number of posts a user answered in a day. We then take the maximum value, but don't partition by anything; we grab it over the entire set. Why are we doing the MAX() in the outermost query then? Well, it's a bit of a hack. We could get the same results either using the MAX() as we have here, or we could NOT use the MAX() and just refer to the column from the second-level query (maxPostsUser), and then we'd also have to add that same column (maxPostsUser) to the GROUP BY clause. I prefer not to add extra columns to the GROUP BY that don't really define the reason for the grouping. Again, though, that's just a personal preference and because I think it makes the intent of the code clearer.

```
, MAX(CASE WHEN secInfo.maxPostsUser = secInfo.numPostsUser THEN secInfo.
DisplayName ELSE NULL END) AS userMostPosts
```

The userMostPosts column returns the DisplayName for the user who has the most responses to posts. We know the value of the maxPostsUser, but we need the associated name. We can do this by finding out the user for whom the numPostsUser equals the maxPostsUser and pull that DisplayName. We're hacking the MAX a bit in this case to help us get the value we want. We do this with a CASE statement, setting the value of the column to NULL when our filter doesn't match: when the maxPostsUser does not equal the numPostsUser. If the two are equivalent, we set the value of the column to the

DisplayName, which will be considered "greater than" NULL and will become the MAX() value for the userMostPosts column.

```
, MAX(CASE WHEN secInfo.maxPostsUser = secInfo.numPostsUser THEN secInfo.
numAccepted ELSE 0 END) AS numAccepted
```

The numAccepted uses a bit of the same "hack" as we used with the userMostPosts. We need to find the number of answers marked as accepted for the user with the highest number of posts. We again use the MAX() with a CASE statement.

```
, MAX(secInfo.numDistinctUsers) AS numUsersResponded
```

The numUsersResponded also doesn't have to be an aggregate, but if we remove the aggregation, we again have to add the column to the GROUP BY. I still prefer the readability that comes with leaving this as an aggregate to keep it (and confusion) out of the GROUP BY.

But What About Performance?

Here's our (and by our, I mean my) STATISTICS IO and TIME output for running the query in Listing 6-7:

```
SQL Server parse and compile time:
   CPU time = 28 ms, elapsed time = 28 ms.
Warning: Null value is eliminated by an aggregate or other SET operation.

(1 row affected)
Table 'Worktable'. Scan count 9, logical reads 103516, physical reads 0,
read-ahead reads 39, lob logical reads 0, lob physical reads 0, lob read-
ahead reads 0.
Table 'Users'. Scan count 0, logical reads 28767, physical reads 0, read-
ahead reads 0, lob logical reads 0, lob physical reads 0, lob read-ahead
reads 0.
Table 'Posts'. Scan count 5575, logical reads 77880, physical reads 0,
read-ahead reads 0, lob logical reads 0, lob physical reads 0, lob read-
ahead reads 0.

 SQL Server Execution Times:
   CPU time = 359 ms,  elapsed time = 688 ms.
```

We're doing a lot of reads, users and posts, but that's to be expected. We're getting 10,000 responses and 5,500 posts, so we're pulling a lot of data and then doing aggregates. We couldn't really get information from the old procedure because with the loops, it had so much output that we couldn't concatenate it effectively. However, this appears to run very quickly.

Let's try to run this for the whole month. We change this

```
WHERE p.CreationDate >= '20120801'
    AND p.CreationDate < '20120802'
```

to

```
WHERE p.CreationDate >= '20120801'
    AND p.CreationDate < '20120901'
```

And add an order by:

```
ORDER BY secInfo.createDate;
```

If we make these changes, we find the code in Listing 6-8. Let's run that code with STATISTICS IO and TIME set to on.

Listing 6-8. Adjusting query in Listing 6-6 to get data for each day for a month

```
SELECT COUNT(secInfo.Id) AS numPosts  -- level three - outermost
            , secInfo.createDate
            , SUM(secInfo.AnswerCount) AS numResponses
            , MAX(secInfo.maxUpvotes) AS numHighestUpvotesOneAnswer
            , MAX(secInfo.maxPostsUser) AS maxPostsuser
            , MAX(CASE WHEN secInfo.maxPostsUser = secInfo.numPostsUser
                THEN secInfo.DisplayName ELSE NULL END) AS userMostPosts
            , MAX(CASE WHEN secInfo.maxPostsUser = secInfo.numPostsUser
                THEN secInfo.numAccepted ELSE 0 END) AS numAccepted
            , MAX(secInfo.numDistinctUsers) AS numUsersResponded
FROM (
SELECT theInfo.Id -- level two
            , theInfo.createDate
            , theInfo.AnswerCount
            , MAX(theInfo.Score) OVER () AS maxUpvotes
```

```
            , MAX(theInfo.numPostsUser) OVER () AS maxPostsUser
            , theInfo.numPostsUser
            , theInfo.DisplayName
            , MAX(theInfo.numUsersPost) OVER () AS maxNumUsersPost
            , theInfo.numAccepted
            , SUM(CASE WHEN theInfo.theUserRowNum = 1 THEN 1 ELSE 0 END)
              OVER () AS numDistinctUsers
            , ROW_NUMBER() OVER (PARTITION BY Id ORDER BY numPostsUser
              DESC) AS theIDRow
FROM (
SELECT p.Id -- level one - innermost
            , CAST(p.CreationDate AS DATE) AS createDate
            , p.AnswerCount
            , pUser.Score
            , COUNT(pUser.ParentId) OVER (PARTITION BY pUser.OwnerUserId)
              AS numPostsUser
            , COUNT(pUser.OwnerUserId) OVER (PARTITION BY pUser.ParentId)
              AS numUsersPost
            , pUser.ParentId
            , pUser.OwnerUserId
            , SUM(CASE WHEN pUser.Id = p.AcceptedAnswerId THEN 1 ELSE 0
              END) OVER (PARTITION BY pUser.OwnerUserId) AS numAccepted
            , u.DisplayName
            , ROW_NUMBER() OVER (PARTITION BY pUser.OwnerUserId ORDER BY
              pUser.ParentId DESC) AS theUserRowNum
FROM dbo.Posts p
      LEFT OUTER JOIN dbo.Posts pUser ON p.Id = pUser.ParentId
            AND EXISTS (SELECT pUser.OwnerUserId EXCEPT (SELECT NULL UNION
            SELECT 0))
            AND pUser.PostTypeId = 2
      LEFT OUTER JOIN dbo.Users u ON pUser.OwnerUserId = u.Id
WHERE p.CreationDate >= '20120801'
      AND p.CreationDate < '20120901'
      AND p.PostTypeId = 1) theInfo

) secInfo
```

```
WHERE secInfo.theIDRow = 1
GROUP BY secInfo.createDate
ORDER BY secInfo.createDate;
```

Hey, it finishes in 1 minute and 36 seconds, which we can see when we look at the STATISTICS IO and TIME output for running the query in Listing 6-8! That's much better than the 41 minutes for the original report. Here is that STATISTICS IO and TIME output:

```
SQL Server parse and compile time:
   CPU time = 15 ms, elapsed time = 28 ms.
Warning: Null value is eliminated by an aggregate or other SET operation.
(30 rows affected)
Table 'Worktable'. Scan count 9, logical reads 2404707, physical reads 0,
read-ahead reads 954, lob logical reads 0, lob physical reads 0, lob read-
ahead reads 0.
Table 'Workfile'. Scan count 0, logical reads 0, physical reads 0, read-
ahead reads 0, lob logical reads 0, lob physical reads 0, lob read-ahead
reads 0.
Table 'Users'. Scan count 1, logical reads 44532, physical reads 0, read-
ahead reads 44476, lob logical reads 0, lob physical reads 0, lob read-
ahead reads 0.
Table 'Posts'. Scan count 2, logical reads 4918239, physical reads 10086,
read-ahead reads 4238568, lob logical reads 0, lob physical reads 0, lob
read-ahead reads 0.
 SQL Server Execution Times:
   CPU time = 62266 ms,  elapsed time = 96953 ms.
```

We are still doing a lot of reads, but again, we're pulling a lot of data. When we check our output, though, we run into a problem. We can see the problem illustrated in Table 6-6.

Table 6-6. Output from query in Listing 6-8

Num Posts	Create Date	Num Responses	Num Highest Upvotes One Answer	maxPosts user	User Most Posts	Num Accepted	numUsers Responded
5574	2012-08-01	10,248	3810	536	Jon Skeet	364	57533
5600	2012-08-02	10,345	3810	536	Jon Skeet	364	57533
5153	2012-08-03	9525	3810	536	Jon Skeet	364	57533
2524	2012-08-04	4,505	3,810	536	Jon Skeet	364	57533
2572	2012-08-05	4,565	3810	536	Jon Skeet	364	57533
5082	2012-08-06	9201	3810	536	Jon Skeet	364	57533
5603	2012-08-07	9,985	3810	536	Jon Skeet	364	57533
5743	2012-08-08	10,510	3810	536	Jon Skeet	364	57533
5708	2012-08-09	10342	3810	536	Jon Skeet	364	57533
5135	2012-08-10	9360	3810	536	Jon Skeet	364	57533
2400	2012-08-11	4204	3810	536	Jon Skeet	364	57533
2554	2012-08-12	4483	3810	536	Jon Skeet	364	57533
5266	2012-08-13	9346	3810	536	Jon Skeet	364	57533
5566	2012-08-14	10154	3810	536	Jon Skeet	364	57533
5000	2012-08-15	8909	3810	536	Jon Skeet	364	57533

(continued)

157

Table 6-6. (*continued*)

Num Posts	Create Date	Num Responses	Num Highest Upvotes One Answer	maxPosts user	User Most Posts	Num Accepted	numUsers Responded
5547	2012-08-16	10009	3810	536	Jon Skeet	364	57533
5017	2012-08-17	9180	3810	536	Jon Skeet	364	57533
2667	2012-08-18	4822	3810	536	Jon Skeet	364	57533
2441	2012-08-19	4294	3810	536	Jon Skeet	364	57533
4903	2012-08-20	8721	3810	536	Jon Skeet	364	57533
5327	2012-08-21	9700	3810	536	Jon Skeet	364	57533
5580	2012-08-22	10060	3810	536	Jon Skeet	364	57533
5643	2012-08-23	10026	3810	536	Jon Skeet	364	57533
5035	2012-08-24	8869	3810	536	Jon Skeet	364	57533
2603	2012-08-25	4639	3810	536	Jon Skeet	364	57533
2551	2012-08-26	4421	3810	536	Jon Skeet	364	57533
5016	2012-08-27	9042	3810	536	Jon Skeet	364	57533
5476	2012-08-28	9877	3810	536	Jon Skeet	364	57533
5721	2012-08-29	10472	3810	536	Jon Skeet	364	57533
5763	2012-08-30	10488	3810	536	Jon Skeet	364	57533
4912	2012-08-31	9064	3810	536	Jon Skeet	364	57533

Our totals are "total" totals (over the entire recordset), not "by day" totals. We can see that illustrated in the numHighestUpvotesOneAnswer, maxPostsUser, userMostPosts, NumAccepted, and numUsersResponded columns. Let's go back and look at our first-level or innermost query from Listing 6-6:

```
SELECT p.Id
    , CAST(p.CreationDate AS DATE) AS createDate
    , p.AnswerCount
    , pUser.Score
    , COUNT(pUser.ParentId) OVER (PARTITION BY pUser.OwnerUserId) AS
      numPostsUser
    , COUNT(pUser.OwnerUserId) OVER (PARTITION BY pUser.ParentId) AS
      numUsersPost
    , pUser.ParentId
    , pUser.OwnerUserId
    , SUM(CASE WHEN pUser.Id = p.AcceptedAnswerId THEN 1 ELSE 0 END) OVER
      (PARTITION BY pUser.OwnerUserId) AS numAccepted
    , u.DisplayName
    , ROW_NUMBER() OVER (PARTITION BY pUser.OwnerUserId ORDER BY pUser.
      ParentId DESC) AS theUserRowNum
FROM dbo.posts p
    LEFT OUTER JOIN dbo.Posts pUser ON p.Id = pUser.ParentId
        AND EXISTS (SELECT pUser.OwnerUserId EXCEPT (SELECT NULL UNION
        SELECT 0))
        AND pUser.PostTypeId = 2
    LEFT OUTER JOIN dbo.Users u ON pUser.OwnerUserId = u.Id
WHERE p.CreationDate >= '20120801'
    AND p.CreationDate < '20120901'
    AND p.PostTypeId = 1
```

Ah-ha! We have four lines where we should partition by the date in addition to other partitioning. Let's add in the date partitions and see if this fixes our issues. The revised query, including date partitioning in the first level, is shown in Listing 6-9. The new partitioning is underlined in the listing.

Listing 6-9. Revising the first-level or innermost query to include date partitioning

```
SELECT COUNT(secInfo.Id) AS numPosts  -- level three - outermost
            , secInfo.createDate
            , SUM(secInfo.AnswerCount) AS numResponses
            , MAX(secInfo.maxUpvotes) AS numHighestUpvotesOneAnswer
            , MAX(secInfo.maxPostsUser) AS maxPostsuser
            , MAX(CASE WHEN secInfo.maxPostsUser = secInfo.numPostsUser
              THEN secInfo.DisplayName ELSE NULL END) AS userMostPosts
            , MAX(CASE WHEN secInfo.maxPostsUser = secInfo.numPostsUser
              THEN secInfo.numAccepted ELSE 0 END) AS numAccepted
            , MAX(secInfo.numDistinctUsers) AS numUsersResponded
FROM (
SELECT theInfo.Id -- level two
            , theInfo.createDate
            , theInfo.AnswerCount
            , MAX(theInfo.Score) OVER () AS maxUpvotes
            , MAX(theInfo.numPostsUser) OVER () AS maxPostsUser
            , theInfo.numPostsUser
            , theInfo.DisplayName
            , MAX(theInfo.numUsersPost) OVER () AS maxNumUsersPost
            , theInfo.numAccepted
            , SUM(CASE WHEN theInfo.theUserRowNum = 1 THEN 1 ELSE 0 END)
              OVER () AS numDistinctUsers
            , ROW_NUMBER() OVER (PARTITION BY Id ORDER BY numPostsUser
              DESC) AS theIDRow
FROM (SELECT p.Id -- level one - innermost
        , CAST(p.CreationDate AS DATE) AS createDate
        , p.AnswerCount
        , pUser.Score
        , COUNT(pUser.ParentId) OVER (PARTITION BY CAST(p.CreationDate AS
          DATE), pUser.OwnerUserId) AS numPostsUser
        , COUNT(pUser.OwnerUserId) OVER (PARTITION BY CAST(p.CreationDate AS
          DATE), pUser.ParentId) AS numUsersPost
        , pUser.ParentId
```

```
    , pUser.OwnerUserId
    , SUM(CASE WHEN pUser.Id = p.AcceptedAnswerId THEN 1 ELSE 0 END) OVER
      (PARTITION BY CAST(p.CreationDate AS DATE), pUser.OwnerUserId) AS
      numAccepted
    , u.DisplayName
    , ROW_NUMBER() OVER (PARTITION BY CAST(p.CreationDate AS DATE),
      pUser.OwnerUserId ORDER BY pUser.ParentId DESC) AS theUserRowNum
FROM dbo.Posts p
      LEFT OUTER JOIN dbo.Posts pUser ON p.Id = pUser.ParentId
            AND EXISTS (SELECT pUser.OwnerUserId EXCEPT (SELECT NULL UNION
            SELECT 0))
      LEFT OUTER JOIN dbo.Users u ON pUser.OwnerUserId = u.Id
WHERE p.CreationDate >= '20120801'
      AND p.CreationDate < '20120901'
      AND p.PostTypeId = 1) theInfo

) secInfo
WHERE secInfo.theIDRow = 1
GROUP BY secInfo.createDate
ORDER BY secInfo.createDate;
```

Are the changes to the innermost level that we detail in Listing 6-9 going to be enough to get us the final output that we want? Let's go ahead and run the code in Listing 6-9 and see. When we review the results, shown in Table 6-7, we see that we are closer but still not exactly correct.

In Table 6-7, we see that our users/posts data is still the same for each day, and we only see the highest user per date on a single row. What else do we need to modify? The initial report output struggled with this as well and didn't end up being correct for each day. Let's go to the second level of the code in Listing 6-9 and see what changes we may need to make. It looks like we can add the date partition at this level as well for the columns we're still having issues with, like the numHighestUpvotesOneAnswer (which is derived from the MaxUpvotes column), maxPostsUser, maxNumUsersPost, numAccepted, and numDistinctusers columns. New date partitioning is underlined in the code in Listing 6-10.

Table 6-7. Results from running code in Listing 6-9

Num Posts	Create Date	Num Responses	Num Highest Upvotes One Answer	Max Posts user	User Most Posts	Num Accepted	numUsers Responded
5574	2012-08-01	10,248	3,810	45	NULL	0	135617
5600	2012-08-02	10,345	3,810	45	NULL	0	135617
5153	2012-08-03	9525	3810	45	NULL	0	135617
2524	2012-08-04	4,505	3,810	45	NULL	0	135617
2572	2012-08-05	4,565	3,810	45	NULL	0	135617
5082	2012-08-06	9201	3810	45	NULL	0	135617
5603	2012-08-07	9,985	3,810	45	NULL	0	135617
5743	2012-08-08	10,510	3,810	45	NULL	0	135617
5708	2012-08-09	10342	3810	45	NULL	0	135617
5135	2012-08-10	9360	3810	45	NULL	0	135617
2400	2012-08-11	4204	3810	45	NULL	0	135617
2554	2012-08-12	4483	3810	45	NULL	0	135617
5266	2012-08-13	9346	3810	45	NULL	0	135617
5566	2012-08-14	10154	3810	45	NULL	0	135617
5000	2012-08-15	8909	3810	45	NULL	0	135617

(continued)

5547	2012-08-16	10009	3810	45	NULL	0	135617
5017	2012-08-17	9180	3810	45	NULL	0	135617
2667	2012-08-18	4822	3810	45	NULL	0	135617
2441	2012-08-19	4294	3810	45	NULL	0	135617
4903	2012-08-20	8721	3810	45	NULL	0	135617
5327	2012-08-21	9700	3810	45	NULL	0	135617
5580	2012-08-22	10060	3810	45	NULL	0	135617
5643	2012-08-23	10026	3810	45	NULL	0	135617
5035	2012-08-24	8869	3810	45	NULL	0	135617
2603	2012-08-25	4639	3810	45	NULL	0	135617
2551	2012-08-26	4421	3810	45	NULL	0	135617
5016	2012-08-27	9042	3810	45	NULL	0	135617
5476	2012-08-28	9877	3810	45	NULL	0	135617
5721	2012-08-29	10472	3810	45	Aghilas Yakoub	6	135617
5763	2012-08-30	10488	3810	45	NULL	0	135617

Listing 6-10. The code in Listing 6-9 with createDate partitioning added to the second level

```
SELECT COUNT(secInfo.Id) AS numPosts  -- level three - outermost
            , secInfo.createDate
            , SUM(secInfo.AnswerCount) AS numResponses
            , MAX(secInfo.maxUpvotes) AS numHighestUpvotesOneAnswer
            , MAX(secInfo.maxPostsUser) AS maxPostsuser
            , MAX(CASE WHEN secInfo.maxPostsUser = secInfo.numPostsUser
              THEN secInfo.DisplayName ELSE NULL END) AS userMostPosts
            , MAX(CASE WHEN secInfo.maxPostsUser = secInfo.numPostsUser
              THEN secInfo.numAccepted ELSE O END) AS numAccepted
            , MAX(secInfo.numDistinctUsers) AS numUsersResponded
FROM (SELECT theInfo.Id -- level two
            , theInfo.createDate
            , MAX(theInfo.AnswerCount) OVER (PARTITION BY theInfo.Id) AS
              answerCount
            , MAX(theInfo.Score) OVER (PARTITION BY theInfo.createDate) AS
              maxUpvotes
            , MAX(theInfo.numPostsUser) OVER (PARTITION BY theInfo.
              createDate) AS maxPostsUser
            , theInfo.numPostsUser
            , theInfo.DisplayName
            , MAX(theInfo.numUsersPost) OVER (PARTITION BY theInfo.
              createDate) AS maxNumUsersPost
            , theInfo.numAccepted
            , SUM(CASE WHEN theInfo.theUserRowNum = 1 THEN 1 ELSE O END)
              OVER (PARTITION BY theInfo.createDate) AS numDistinctUsers
            , ROW_NUMBER() OVER (PARTITION BY Id ORDER BY numPostsUser
              DESC) AS theIDRow
FROM (
SELECT p.Id
            , CAST(p.CreationDate AS DATE) AS createDate
            , p.AnswerCount
            , pUser.Score
```

```
        , COUNT(pUser.ParentId) OVER (PARTITION BY CAST(p.CreationDate
            AS DATE), pUser.OwnerUserId) AS numPostsUser
        , COUNT(pUser.OwnerUserId) OVER (PARTITION BY CAST(p.
            CreationDate AS DATE), pUser.ParentId) AS numUsersPost
        , pUser.ParentId
        , pUser.OwnerUserId
        , SUM(CASE WHEN pUser.Id = p.AcceptedAnswerId THEN 1 ELSE 0
            END) OVER (PARTITION BY CAST(p.CreationDate AS DATE), pUser.
            OwnerUserId) AS numAccepted
        , u.DisplayName
        , ROW_NUMBER() OVER (PARTITION BY CAST(p.CreationDate AS
            DATE), pUser.OwnerUserId ORDER BY pUser.ParentId DESC) AS
            theUserRowNum
FROM dbo.Posts p
    LEFT OUTER JOIN dbo.Posts pUser ON p.Id = pUser.ParentId
            AND EXISTS (SELECT pUser.OwnerUserId EXCEPT (SELECT NULL UNION
            SELECT 0))
            AND pUser.PostTypeId = 2
    LEFT OUTER JOIN dbo.Users u ON pUser.OwnerUserId = u.Id
WHERE p.CreationDate >= '20120801'
    AND p.CreationDate < '20120901'
    AND p. PostTypeId = 1
) theInfo
) secInfo
WHERE secInfo.theIDRow = 1
GROUP BY secInfo.createDate
ORDER BY secInfo.createDate;
```

Did this level of added partitioning help distribute the data more correctly? When we run the code in Listing 6-10, we see the results illustrated in Table 6-8.

Table 6-8. *Results from running code in Listing 6-10*

Num Posts	Create Date	Num Responses	Num Highest Upvotes One Answer	maxPosts user	User Most Posts	Num Accepted	Num Users Responded
5574	2012-08-01	10,248	1,179	25	Jon Skeet	16	5506
5600	2012-08-02	10,345	483	28	Jon Skeet	21	5462
5153	2012-08-03	9525	370	33	Jon Skeet	19	5093
2524	2012-08-04	4,505	401	22	Bergi	11	2618
2572	2012-08-05	4,565	495	25	Bergi	9	2555
5082	2012-08-06	9201	3810	31	Peter Lawrey	13	5042
5603	2012-08-07	9,985	462	22	Gordon Linoff	4	5417
5743	2012-08-08	10,510	1,066	34	Peter Lawrey	13	5522
5708	2012-08-09	10342	508	41	Peter Lawrey	13	5540
5135	2012-08-10	9360	356	26	Peter Lawrey	12	5033
2400	2012-08-11	4204	446	19	Mohammod Hossain	3	2439
2554	2012-08-12	4483	887	16	Nicholas Albion	4	2572
5266	2012-08-13	9346	479	32	Mike Brant	6	5129
5566	2012-08-14	10154	628	38	Darin Dimitrov	21	5363
5000	2012-08-15	8909	482	29	Darin Dimitrov	22	4754

(continued)

5547	2012-08-16	10009	628	26	nandeesh	19	5376
5017	2012-08-17	9180	594	27	Darin Dimitrov	19	4964
2667	2012-08-18	4822	182	31	Hassan Boutougha	5	2687
2441	2012-08-19	4294	455	24	ronalchn	10	2436
4903	2012-08-20	8721	238	23	Gordon Linoff	6	4845
5327	2012-08-21	9700	721	31	Peter Lawrey	15	5280
5580	2012-08-22	10060	430	37	Jon Skeet	17	5508
5643	2012-08-23	10026	594	28	Jon Skeet	17	5412
5035	2012-08-24	8869	316	24	Alex Coleman	7	4808
2603	2012-08-25	4639	513	19	nneonneo	11	2576
2551	2012-08-26	4421	1486	35	TheHe	15	2467
5016	2012-08-27	9042	1577	26	Jon Hanna	15	4929
5476	2012-08-28	9877	348	27	Aghilas Yakoub	4	5308
5721	2012-08-29	10472	2190	45	Aghilas Yakoub	6	5445
5763	2012-08-30	10488	611	38	Peter Lawrey	17	5531
4912	2012-08-31	9064	507	33	Peter Lawrey	17	4783

The results in Table 6-8 look much better, but it's probably time for another sanity check. I may just run this for a few single days to check the "duplicates" we see, such as Peter Lawrey being the user with the most posts on August 8–10, to verify if those results are correct. Let's go with August 8–10 to see if we get Peter Lawrey as the user with the most post responses. Our results are shown in the result sets in Table 6-9.

Table 6-9. *Results from running code in Listing 6-10 for 8/8/2012, 8/9/2012, and 8/10/2012*

Num Posts	Create Date	Num Responses	Num Highest Upvotes One Answer	Max Posts user	userMost Posts	Num Accepted	numUsers Responded
5743	2012-08-08	10510	1066	34	Peter Lawrey	13	5522
5708	2012-08-09	10,342	508	41	Peter Lawrey	13	5540
5135	2012-08-10	9,360	356	26	Peter Lawrey	12	5033

The results from the three queries run, shown in Table 6-9, verify the results we got when running the query in Listing 6-10 for an entire month. Our numbers are looking much more correct, and the runtimes are down to almost nothing – for a single day, the query in Listing 6-10 is running in 1 second. For a month, it's running in about a minute and a half, as opposed to over 40 minutes!

What data are we still missing that the original report had? The columns we haven't accounted for yet are DayofWeek, DayofMonth, and the percentage of posts. Unfortunately, the percentage of posts metric is ridiculous; it's always going to be so small as to be almost negligible. Consider the August 10th results from Table 6-9. The metric value would equal 26/9360, which will be an extremely tiny number. However, we'll put this column in our set of results, because the original functionality includes that metric.

Also, let's make sure we're outputting the columns in the same order with the same names, in order to avoid potential report changes on the application or reporting side. We never did have the number of accepted answers by that highest user on that day in the original output, but it was in the spec, so we'll leave it as the last column in case someone wants to add it to the report. If the column causes issues there, we can always comment it out if need be in the final output. When we add all the code for these additional values, we get the query in Listing 6-11.

Listing 6-11. Final code to replace original dailySummaryReportByMonth stored procedure code

```
SELECT secInfo.createDate AS monthYear
      , DATEPART(dd, secInfo.CreateDate) AS [dayOfMonth]
      , DATEPART(dw, secInfo.createDate) AS [dayOfWeek]
      , COUNT(secInfo.Id) AS numPosts
      , SUM(secInfo.AnswerCount) AS numResponses
      , MAX(secInfo.numDistinctUsers) AS numUsersResponded
      , MAX(secInfo.maxPostsUser) AS highNumUsersSinglePost
      , MAX(CASE WHEN secInfo.maxPostsUser = secInfo.numPostsUser THEN
        secInfo.DisplayName ELSE NULL END) AS userMostResponses
      , CAST(MAX(secInfo.maxPostsUser)/COUNT(secInfo.Id) * 100 AS
        DECIMAL(8,7)) AS percentagePosts
      , MAX(secInfo.maxUpvotes) AS numHighestUpvotesOneAnswer
      , MAX(CASE WHEN secInfo.maxPostsUser = secInfo.numPostsUser THEN
        secInfo.numAccepted ELSE 0 END) AS numAccepted

FROM (
SELECT theInfo.Id
      , theInfo.createDate
      , theInfo.AnswerCount
      , MAX(theInfo.Score) OVER (PARTITION BY theInfo.createDate) AS
        maxUpvotes
      , MAX(theInfo.numPostsUser) OVER (PARTITION BY theInfo.createDate) AS
        maxPostsUser
      , theInfo.numPostsUser
      , theInfo.DisplayName
      , MAX(theInfo.numUsersPost) OVER (PARTITION BY theInfo.createDate) AS
        maxNumUsersPost
      , theInfo.numAccepted
      , SUM(CASE WHEN theInfo.theUserRowNum = 1 THEN 1 ELSE 0 END) OVER
        (PARTITION BY theInfo.createDate) AS numDistinctUsers
      , ROW_NUMBER() OVER (PARTITION BY Id ORDER BY numPostsUser DESC) AS
        theIDRow
FROM (
```

```
        SELECT p.Id
                , CAST(p.CreationDate AS DATE) AS createDate
                , p.AnswerCount
                , pUser.Score
                , COUNT(pUser.ParentId) OVER (PARTITION BY CAST(p.CreationDate
                    AS DATE), pUser.OwnerUserId) AS numPostsUser
                , COUNT(pUser.OwnerUserId) OVER (PARTITION BY CAST(p.
                    CreationDate AS DATE), pUser.ParentId) AS numUsersPost
                , pUser.ParentId
                , pUser.OwnerUserId
                , SUM(CASE WHEN pUser.Id = p.AcceptedAnswerId THEN 1 ELSE 0
                    END) OVER (PARTITION BY CAST(p.CreationDate AS DATE), pUser.
                    OwnerUserId) AS numAccepted
                , u.DisplayName
                , ROW_NUMBER() OVER (PARTITION BY CAST(p.CreationDate AS
                    DATE), pUser.OwnerUserId ORDER BY pUser.ParentId DESC) AS
                    theUserRowNum
FROM dbo.Posts p
        LEFT OUTER JOIN dbo.Posts pUser ON p.Id = pUser.ParentId
                AND EXISTS (SELECT pUser.OwnerUserId EXCEPT (SELECT NULL UNION
                    SELECT 0))
                AND pUser.PostTypeId = 2
        LEFT OUTER JOIN dbo.Users u ON pUser.OwnerUserId = u.Id
WHERE p.CreationDate >= '20120801'
        AND p.CreationDate < '20120901'
        AND p.PostTypeId = 1
) theInfo

) secInfo
WHERE secInfo.theIDRow = 1
GROUP BY secInfo.createDate
ORDER BY secInfo.createDate;
```

No Missing Rows – Tally Tables!

We need to put it back into the framework of a stored procedure. And what if there are no posts in a day? We'd be missing lines, and we might get a divide-by-zero error. It would be unlikely that this would happen, but we could use a numbers or tally table to make sure that we get a row for every day whether there are posts or not. A numbers table is simply a table with a single incrementing integer column with a primary key/clustered index that allows you to "iterate" in a set-based way. Our numbers table in this database is dbo.Numbers and contains 5 million rows.

We want to make our query from Listing 6-11 a LEFT OUTER JOIN to our Numbers table, so we definitely get one row returned for every date even if there is no data in that row. We need to then make sure we group on our Numbers record instead of the code in Listing 6-11, because if you leave references to the LEFT OUTER JOIN in the WHERE clause and your GROUP BY, it will get treated as an INNER JOIN, and you'll still lose the rows we're trying to avoid by using the Numbers table. Let's run the code in Listing 6-12.

Listing 6-12. Code over dates without posts

```
SELECT COUNT(1) as numPosts
, CAST(CreationDate AS DATE) AS theDate
FROM dbo.Posts
WHERE CreationDate >= '20080715'
    AND CreationDate < '20080816'
GROUP BY CAST(CreationDate AS DATE)
ORDER BY CAST(CreationDate AS DATE);
```

The output of this query is shown in Table 6-10. We're missing the dates from 7/15/2008 until 7/31/2008 (the minimum creationdate in the table). However, we can use the Numbers table to show these dates even though there are no posts.

Table 6-10. *Results from the code in Listing 6-12*

numPosts	theDate
6	2008-07-31
140	2008-08-01
94	2008-08-02
132	2008-08-03
326	2008-08-04
515	2008-08-05
504	2008-08-06
588	2008-08-07
448	2008-08-08
231	2008-08-09
188	2008-08-10
454	2008-08-11
553	2008-08-12
526	2008-08-13
633	2008-08-14
593	2008-08-15

Listing 6-13. Showing dates without posts using the Numbers table

```
DECLARE @numDays tinyint = DATEDIFF(dd, '20080715', '20080816');
SELECT COALESCE(numPosts,0) AS numPosts
         , DATEADD(dd, n-1, '20080715') AS theDate
         , num.n
FROM dbo.numbers num
LEFT OUTER JOIN (SELECT COUNT(1) as numPosts
, CAST(creationdate AS date) AS theDate
FROM dbo.Posts
WHERE CreationDate >= '20080715'
```

```
    AND CreationDate < '20080816'
GROUP BY CAST(CreationDate AS DATE)
) postInfo ON DATEADD(dd, n-1, '20080715') = postInfo.theDate
WHERE num.n <= @numdays
ORDER BY num.n;
```

The code in Listing 6-13 shows us how, by using the Numbers table, we cause a record to be generated for each date whether or not there are posts on those dates. We might get the numPosts equal to 0, but this is the correct count of posts for that day! We can see the results in Table 6-11.

Table 6-11. *The results of the code from Listing 6-13*

numPosts	theDate
0	2008-07-15 0:00:00
0	2008-07-16 0:00:00
0	2008-07-17 0:00:00
0	2008-07-18 0:00:00
0	2008-07-19 0:00:00
0	2008-07-20 0:00:00
0	2008-07-21 0:00:00
0	2008-07-22 0:00:00
0	2008-07-23 0:00:00
0	2008-07-24 0:00:00
0	2008-07-25 0:00:00
0	2008-07-26 0:00:00
0	2008-07-27 0:00:00
0	2008-07-28 0:00:00
0	2008-07-29 0:00:00
0	2008-07-30 0:00:00

(*continued*)

Table 6-11. (*continued*)

numPosts	theDate
6	2008-07-31 0:00:00
140	2008-08-01 0:00:00
94	2008-08-02 0:00:00
132	2008-08-03 0:00:00
326	2008-08-04 0:00:00
515	2008-08-05 0:00:00
504	2008-08-06 0:00:00
588	2008-08-07 0:00:00
448	2008-08-08 0:00:00
231	2008-08-09 0:00:00
188	2008-08-10 0:00:00
454	2008-08-11 0:00:00
553	2008-08-12 0:00:00
526	2008-08-13 0:00:00
633	2008-08-14 0:00:00
593	2008-08-15 0:00:00

We want to keep the code that adjusted if the date passed in wasn't the first day of the month, so we will include those adjustments in our new version. With the addition of the stored procedure wrapper code and the Numbers table code, our new version of the DailySummaryReportPerMonth stored procedure is complete and shown in Listing 6-14.

Listing 6-14. Final version, replacement code for DailySummaryReportPerMonth

```
ALTER PROCEDURE [dbo].[DailySummaryReportPerMonth] @monthyear DATETIME2
AS
        /* in case the first day of the month not passed in */
```

```
     SET @monthyear = DATEADD(month, DATEDIFF(month, 0, @monthYear), 0);
DECLARE @enddate datetime2 = DATEADD(month, 1, @monthYear);
DECLARE @numDays tinyint = DATEDIFF(dd, @monthYear, @enddate);

SELECT  DATEADD(dd,num.n-1,@monthYear) AS monthYear
      , DATEPART(dd, DATEADD(dd,num.n-1,@monthYear)) AS [dayOfMonth]
      , DATEPART(dw, DATEADD(dd, num.n-1,@monthYear)) AS [dayOfWeek]
      , COUNT(secInfo.Id) AS numPosts
      , SUM(secInfo.AnswerCount) AS numResponses
      , MAX(secInfo.numDistinctUsers) AS numUsersResponded
      , MAX(secInfo.maxPostsUser) AS highNumUsersSinglePost
      , MAX(CASE WHEN secInfo.maxPostsUser = secInfo.numPostsUser THEN
        secInfo.DisplayName ELSE NULL END) AS userMostResponses
      , CAST(MAX(secInfo.maxPostsUser)/COUNT(secInfo.Id) * 100 AS
        DECIMAL(8,7)) AS percentagePosts
      , MAX(secInfo.maxUpvotes) AS numHighestUpvotesOneAnswer
      , MAX(CASE WHEN secInfo.maxPostsUser = secInfo.numPostsUser THEN
        secInfo.numAccepted ELSE 0 END) AS numAccepted
FROM dbo.Numbers num
LEFT OUTER JOIN (
        SELECT theInfo.Id
              , theInfo.createDate
              , MAX(theInfo.AnswerCount) OVER (PARTITION BY theInfo.ID) AS
                answerCount
              , MAX(theInfo.Score) OVER (PARTITION BY theInfo.createDate) AS
                maxUpvotes
              , MAX(theInfo.numPostsUser) OVER (PARTITION BY theInfo.
                createDate) AS maxPostsUser
              , theInfo.numPostsUser
              , theInfo.DisplayName
              , MAX(theInfo.numUsersPost) OVER (PARTITION BY theInfo.
                createDate) AS maxNumUsersPost
              , theInfo.numAccepted
              , SUM(CASE WHEN theInfo.theUserRowNum = 1 THEN 1 ELSE 0 END)
                OVER (PARTITION BY theInfo.createDate) AS numDistinctUsers
```

175

```
            , ROW_NUMBER() OVER (PARTITION BY Id ORDER BY numPostsUser
              DESC) AS theIDRow
    FROM (
        SELECT p.Id
                , CAST(p.CreationDate AS DATE) AS createDate
                , p.AnswerCount
                , pUser.Score
                , COUNT(pUser.ParentId) OVER (PARTITION BY CAST(p.
                  CreationDate AS DATE), pUser.OwnerUserId) AS numPostsUser
                , COUNT(pUser.OwnerUserId) OVER (PARTITION BY CAST(p.
                  CreationDate AS DATE), pUser.ParentId) AS numUsersPost
                , pUser.ParentId
                , pUser.OwnerUserId
                , SUM(CASE WHEN pUser.Id = p.AcceptedAnswerId THEN 1
                  ELSE 0 END) OVER (PARTITION BY CAST(p.CreationDate AS
                  DATE), pUser.OwnerUserId) AS numAccepted
                , u.DisplayName
                , ROW_NUMBER() OVER (PARTITION BY CAST(p.CreationDate AS
                  DATE), pUser.OwnerUserId ORDER BY pUser.ParentId DESC)
                  AS theUserRowNum
        FROM dbo.Posts p
        LEFT OUTER JOIN dbo.Posts pUser ON p.Id = pUser.ParentId
                AND EXISTS (SELECT pUser.OwnerUserId EXCEPT (SELECT NULL
                UNION SELECT 0))
                AND pUser.PostTypeId = 2
        LEFT OUTER JOIN dbo.Users u ON pUser.OwnerUserId = u.Id
        WHERE p.CreationDate >= @monthYear
                AND p.CreationDate < @endDate
                AND p.PostTypeId = 1
    ) theInfo
) secInfo ON secInfo.createDate = DATEADD(dd, num.n-1,@monthYear) -- n
starts at 1 so you want to subtract one to start with the "normal" first day
    AND secInfo.theIDRow = 1
GROUP BY num.n
ORDER BY num.n;
```

This rewrite ended up being simple. We fixed a couple of other problems besides just removing the loops, but the performance gain can be almost entirely attributed to the loop removal. Also, if you noticed, we added an end date parameter so we could do the correct calculation for the number of days to limit the Numbers table and get our correct number of days for any given month.

What Else Should We Watch For?

Let's take a look at a slightly different example. We have a stored procedure that lets us find information about a user by their user name, or a part of the user name. Say we want to get information about any users with a display name containing the text "Joel". Let's run through our documentation exercise against the getUserInfoByName stored procedure and see what we come up with!

GetUserInfoByName: Documentation
Code as of 2019.07.07

```
IF NOT EXISTS
(
    SELECT 1
    FROM sys.procedures
    WHERE name = 'getUserInfoByName'
)
 BEGIN
    DECLARE @SQL NVARCHAR(1200);
    SET @SQL = N'/
************************************************************************
    2019.07.07          LBohm        INITIAL STORED PROC STUB CREATE RELEASE
************************************************************************/

CREATE PROCEDURE dbo.getUserInfoByName
AS
    SET NOCOUNT ON;
```

```
BEGIN
 SELECT 1;
 END;';
     EXECUTE SP_EXECUTESQL
          @sQL;
END;
GO

/**************************************************************************
Description: Data for users by name
--Test call:
-- EXECUTE dbo.getUserInfoByName @theName = 'Joel';

   2019.07.07          LBohm            INITIAL RELEASE
**************************************************************************/

ALTER PROCEDURE [dbo].[getUserInfoByName] @theName varchar(20)
AS

SELECT u.Id
     , u.DisplayName
     , u.AboutMe
     , count(p.Id) AS numPosts
     , (SELECT COUNT(v.Id) FROM Votes v
          WHERE EXISTS (SELECT 1 FROM Posts vp
                WHERE vp.Id = v.PostId
                      AND vp.OwnerUserId = u.Id)
                      AND v.VoteTypeId = 5) AS numfavVotes
     , (SELECT COUNT(pc.Id)
          FROM dbo.Posts pc
          WHERE pc.OwnerUserId = u.Id
                AND pc.PostTypeId = 2) AS numComments
     , (SELECT MAX(CreationDate)
          FROM dbo.Posts plastcom
          WHERE plastcom.OwnerUserId = u.Id
                AND plastcom.PostTypeId = 2) AS dateLastComment
     , u.UpVotes
```

```
        , u.DownVotes
        , dbo.getlastBadgeUser(u.Id) AS latestBadge
FROM dbo.Users u
        INNER JOIN dbo.Posts p on u.Id = p.OwnerUserId
WHERE u.[DisplayName] LIKE '%' + @theName + '%'
        and p.PostTypeId = 1
GROUP BY u.ID, u.DisplayName, u.AboutMe, u.UpVotes, u.DownVotes;
```

Functional Requirements

- Return from the Users table:

- Id, DisplayName, AboutMe, UpVotes, DownVotes

- Return number of posts from the user with PostTypeId of 1.

- Return number of posts from the user with PostTypeId of 2.

- Return date of the last comment post.

- Return name of the latest badge the user received.

- Filter by the input being somewhere in the displayname.

Data Calls

Table	Operation	Columns Returned	Filtering
dbo.Users	SELECT	Id, DisplayName, AboutMe, UpVotes, DownVotes	DisplayName LIKE %input%
		GROUP BY Id, DisplayName, AboutMe, Upvotes, DownVotes	
dbo.Posts	SELECT	COUNT(Id)	OwnerUserId = User Id, PostTypeId = 1
	EXISTS		OwnerUserId = User Id
	SELECT	COUNT(Id)	OwnerUserId = User Id, PostTypeId = 2

(continued)

Table	Operation	Columns Returned	Filtering
	SELECT	MAX(CreationDate)	OwnerUserId = User Id, PostTypeId = 2
dbo.Votes	SELECT	COUNT(Id)	Id = PostId
function		dbo.getLastBadgeUser(Id)	

Possible Red Flags

Datatype Matching

The input variable is a varchar(20), and the field is an nvarchar(40).

Subqueries

There are three subqueries in the select statement of the only data call. All of them reference the Posts table.

Calculations

N/A

Temporary Tables and/or Table Variables

N/A

Loops/Cursors

N/A

CTEs

N/A

Join Types

Standard

IN/NOT IN/LIKE

LIKE in WHERE clause with both leading and trailing %. Cannot use an index...

Sorting Operations

Large grouping operation

Calls to Other User-Defined SQL Objects

Calls function dbo.getLastBadgeUser

Native SQL Functions in WHERE Clauses

N/A

Run Statistics for This Call

We need to find out what is taking a long time with this query. Let's start by looking at STATISTICS IO and TIME information for a call to this stored procedure using the code in Listing 6-15.

Listing 6-15. Executing the stored procedure with STATISTICS IO and TIME on

```
SET STATISTICS IO,TIME ON;
GO
EXECUTE getUserInfoByName @theName = 'Joel';
```

The STATISTICS IO and TIME output in the Messages tab shows a pretty significant run time, as well as a lot of reads. An hour and 18 minutes is pretty excessive for anything to run, let alone a relatively simple query.

```
SQL Server parse and compile time:
   CPU time = 31 ms, elapsed time = 32 ms.
 SQL Server Execution Times:
   CPU time = 0 ms,  elapsed time = 0 ms.
(666 rows affected)
```

Table 'Posts'. Scan count 1334, logical reads 141862, physical reads 6898, read-ahead reads 25451, lob logical reads 0, lob physical reads 0, lob read-ahead reads 0.
Table 'Workfile'. Scan count 0, logical reads 0, physical reads 0, read-ahead reads 0, lob logical reads 0, lob physical reads 0, lob read-ahead reads 0.
Table 'Worktable'. Scan count 0, logical reads 0, physical reads 0, read-ahead reads 0, lob logical reads 0, lob physical reads 0, lob read-ahead reads 0.
Table 'Votes'. Scan count 666, logical reads 162302868, physical reads 0, read-ahead reads 0, lob logical reads 0, lob physical reads 0, lob read-ahead reads 0.
Table 'Users'. Scan count 1, logical reads 44532, physical reads 0, read-ahead reads 24519, lob logical reads 0, lob physical reads 0, lob read-ahead reads 0.
 SQL Server Execution Times:
   CPU time = 4657469 ms, elapsed time = 4687108 ms.

What seems to be the biggest issue? The several calls to the Posts table being made through both a join and subqueries is a concern. Why would we continue looking up the same general data against that table time and again? We can see how many scans are being done on the Posts table. And whoosh, what about the ridiculous number of reads against the Votes table?

Functions and STATISTICS IO Output

Do you notice anything odd here though? In this output, we don't see any record for reads against the Badges table, and yet our output contains badge information. STATISTICS IO output does not include the work for functions! This is something to definitely be aware of. You can catch that information in a Profiler trace (but who uses them anymore anyway?). You can also catch that information using Extended Events, which is a generally low-cost way (in terms of affecting server performance) to grab the data we need.

Coming Up with a Plan of Action

The issue with this stored procedure seems to be the massive amount of data that is being read, even though that amount of data isn't being returned. Let's see if we can reduce the amount of data getting read by getting rid of

1. The subqueries

2. The function

3. The leading '%' in our LIKE statement

If a LIKE statement only has a trailing '%' and not a leading '%', it can use an index. With the leading '%', though, it cannot use an index.

Go Away, Subqueries!

We identified the Votes table as having massive amounts of reads. Let's try moving the subquery calling the Votes table to a LEFT OUTER JOIN statement instead. In order to get rid of the subqueries to the Posts table, though, we're going to have to be a little tricky and use aggregates and a GROUP BY. We already join to the Posts table, so we have the information available. We need a COUNT() of the post IDs where the PostTypeId = 2, and we also need the MAX() of the creationDate for post IDs where the PostTypeId = 2. This sounds like we're going to need some CASE statements, since in our INNER JOIN we don't specify the PostTypeId. Listing 6-16 shows the modified query with the subqueries removed as we just discussed.

Listing 6-16. getUserInfoByName query with subqueries removed

```
DECLARE @theName NVARCHAR(40) = 'Joel';
SELECT u.Id
    , u.DisplayName
    , u.AboutMe
    , SUM(CASE WHEN p.PostTypeId = 1 THEN 1 ELSE 0 END) AS numPosts
    , SUM(CASE WHEN v.Id IS NOT NULL THEN 1 ELSE 0 END) AS numFavVotes
    , SUM(CASE WHEN p.PostTypeId = 2 THEN 1 ELSE 0 END) AS numComments
    , MAX(CASE WHEN p.PostTypeId = 2 THEN p.CreationDate ELSE '20000101'
      END) AS dateLastComment
    , u.UpVotes
```

183

```
        , u.DownVotes
        , dbo.getlastBadgeUser(u.Id) AS latestBadge
FROM dbo.Users u
INNER JOIN dbo.Posts p ON u.Id = p.OwnerUserId
        LEFT OUTER JOIN dbo.Votes v ON p.Id = v.PostId
            AND v.VoteTypeId = 5
WHERE p.PostTypeId IN (1,2)
 AND u.[DisplayName] LIKE '%' + @theName + '%'
GROUP BY u.Id
        , u.DisplayName
        , u.AboutMe
        , u.UpVotes
        , u.DownVotes
        , dbo.getlastBadgeUser(u.Id);
```

The first step is to run this code with STATISTICS IO and TIME on to see if we're making progress in reducing our reads. The output from the STATISTICS IO and TIME from the query in Listing 6-16, still running against @theName = 'Joel', gives us interesting results:

```
SQL Server parse and compile time:
   CPU time = 15 ms, elapsed time = 18 ms.

 SQL Server Execution Times:
   CPU time = 0 ms,  elapsed time = 0 ms.
```

```
(920 rows affected)
Table 'Worktable'. Scan count 0, logical reads 0, physical reads 0, read-
ahead reads 0, lob logical reads 0, lob physical reads 0, lob read-ahead
reads 0.
Table 'Workfile'. Scan count 2, logical reads 640, physical reads 15, read-
ahead reads 625, lob logical reads 0, lob physical reads 0, lob read-ahead
reads 0.
Table 'Posts'. Scan count 2644, logical reads 142015, physical reads 0,
read-ahead reads 228392, lob logical reads 0, lob physical reads 0, lob
read-ahead reads 0.
```

Table 'Users'. Scan count 1, logical reads 44532, physical reads 0, read-ahead reads 30113, lob logical reads 0, lob physical reads 0, lob read-ahead reads 0.
Table 'Votes'. Scan count 1, logical reads 243698, physical reads 4, read-ahead reads 243476, lob logical reads 0, lob physical reads 0, lob read-ahead reads 0.

SQL Server Execution Times:
  CPU time = 34746844 ms, elapsed time = 34809302 ms.

Running this as a query, not as a stored procedure, showed a significantly longer runtime of over 9 hours, as we see from the output. However, we did reduce our reads by quite a bit. The reduced reads are good, but not at the expense of adding 8 hours to the runtime. Let's see if we can make other changes that will bring the runtime down.

Remove the Function!

The next step is to look at the code in the function and see if we can replace the entire function in the query. The code for creating the function is shown in Listing 6-17.

Listing 6-17. Create statement for dbo.getLastBadgeUser

```
/**************************************************************************
  Object Description: Get latest badge for a userid

  Revision History:
  Date          Name              Label/PTS     Description
  ----------    ---------------   ----------    ------------------------------
  2019.07.07    LBohm                           Initial Release
 **************************************************************************/
CREATE FUNCTION dbo.getLastBadgeUser (@userID int)
RETURNS nvarchar(40)
AS
BEGIN
DECLARE @badgename nvarchar(40);
```

```
SET @badgename = COALESCE((SELECT TOP 1 [Name]
  FROM dbo.Badges
  WHERE userID = @userID
ORDER BY [Date] DESC),"));

RETURN @badgename;
END;
```

We should be able to use an OUTER APPLY with the badge info and move the code from the function almost intact into the OUTER APPLY, as shown in Listing 6-18.

Listing 6-18. The OUTER APPLY to replace the getLastBadgeUser function

```
OUTER APPLY (SELECT TOP 1 [Name] AS latestBadge
        FROM dbo.Badges
        WHERE userID = u.id
        ORDER BY [Date] DESC) AS bInfo
```

Remove the Leading % in Our LIKE Statement

This is the last piece we are going to change in our getUserInfoByName query. As we discussed before, the Query Optimizer can't use an index when there's a leading % in our LIKE statement. Why is this? Well, it makes complete sense if we think about what an index is. It is the data displayed in a certain order. If the leading column is a varchar or similar datatype, the order is alphabetical. If we know the start of the phrase, we can use the index to go find the data which matches the beginning, because we know exactly where in the index it is due to the index's order. If we do not know the beginning, though, we will still have to scan the entire index as opposed to being able to use a targeted seek operation.

When we put our three changes together – removing the subqueries, removing the functions, and removing our leading % in our LIKE statement – we get the code shown in Listing 6-19.

Listing 6-19. Rewrite of the getUserInfoByName stored procedure

```
IF NOT EXISTS
(
     SELECT 1
     FROM sys.procedures
     WHERE name = 'getUserInfoByName'
)
BEGIN
     DECLARE @sQL NVARCHAR(1200);
     SET @sQL = N'
/*****************************************************************
    2019.07.07          LBohm          INITIAL STORED PROC STUB CREATE RELEASE
*****************************************************************/

CREATE PROCEDURE dbo.getUserInfoByName
AS
     SET NOCOUNT ON;

BEGIN
 SELECT 1;
 END;';
     EXECUTE SP_EXECUTESQL
          @sQL;
END;
GO

/*****************************************************************
Description: Data for users by name
--Test call:
-- EXECUTE dbo.getUserInfoByName @theName = 'Joel';

    2019.07.07          LBohm          INITIAL RELEASE
*****************************************************************/

ALTER PROCEDURE [dbo].[getUserInfoByName] @theName varchar(20)
AS
```

```
SELECT u.ID
      , u.displayname
      , u.aboutme
      , SUM(CASE WHEN p.postTypeID = 1 THEN 1 ELSE 0 END) AS numPosts
      , SUM(CASE WHEN v.id IS NOT NULL THEN 1 ELSE 0 END) AS numFavVotes
      , SUM(CASE WHEN p.postTypeID = 2 THEN 1 ELSE 0 END) AS numComments
      , MAX(CASE WHEN p.postTypeID = 2 THEN p.creationDate ELSE '20000101'
        END) AS dateLastComment
      , u.upvotes
      , u.downvotes
      , binfo.latestBadge
FROM dbo.users u
INNER JOIN dbo.posts p ON u.id = p.ownerUserID
      LEFT OUTER JOIN dbo.votes v ON p.ID = v.postID
                        AND v.VoteTypeId = 5
      OUTER APPLY (SELECT TOP 1 [Name] AS latestBadge
              FROM dbo.Badges
              WHERE userID = u.id
              ORDER BY [Date] DESC) AS bInfo
WHERE p.postTypeID IN (1,2)
 AND u.[DisplayName] LIKE @theName + '%'
GROUP BY u.id
              , u.displayname
              , u.aboutme
              , u.upvotes
              , u.downvotes
              , binfo.latestBadge;
```

We need to test both the output and the STATISTICS IO and TIME for this query. After updating the stored procedure definition by running the code in Listing 6-19, we can re-rerun the sample call to this procedure which is found in Listing 6-15. We can then review the results, a subset of which is shown in Table 6-12.

Table 6-12. *Subset of results from running Listing 6-15 against the proc in Listing 6-19*

ID	Display name	numPosts	Num FavVotes	Num Comments	Up votes	Down votes	Latest Badge
673726	Joel	61	26	74	136	16	Notable Question
1267542	Joel	0	0	5	11	0	Analytical
1401298	joel garringer	0	0	1	0	0	Teacher
5416	Joel Martinez	352	297	758	1146	75	asp.net
371344	Joel Spadin	1	0	7	4	0	Supporter
2456626	Joel	4	0	0	5	0	Teacher
1518500	Joell Lapitan	0	0	1	0	0	NULL
766590	joelennon	0	0	1	1	0	Autobiographer
2457739	Joel	1	0	0	0	0	Student
512776	Joel R	6	1	1	3	0	Editor

The STATISTICS IO and TIME output from running the code in Listing 6-15 against the proc in Listing 6-19 shows fewer reads, although there are still fairly high numbers. However, the code is running in about a minute (which is a pretty big gain over the hour it was taking to run):

```
SQL Server parse and compile time:
   CPU time = 0 ms, elapsed time = 0 ms.
SQL Server parse and compile time:
   CPU time = 0 ms, elapsed time = 0 ms.
(876 rows affected)
Table 'Worktable'. Scan count 42764, logical reads 24644589, physical reads
0, read-ahead reads 0, lob logical reads 0, lob physical reads 0, lob read-
ahead reads 0.
Table 'Workfile'. Scan count 0, logical reads 0, physical reads 0, read-ahead
reads 0, lob logical reads 0, lob physical reads 0, lob read-ahead reads 0.
Table 'Badges'. Scan count 1, logical reads 49649, physical reads 0, read-ahead
reads 0, lob logical reads 0, lob physical reads 0, lob read-ahead reads 0.
```

```
Table 'Votes'. Scan count 1, logical reads 243698, physical reads 0, read-
ahead reads 177026, lob logical reads 0, lob physical reads 0, lob read-
ahead reads 0.
Table 'Posts'. Scan count 2458, logical reads 97205, physical reads 232,
read-ahead reads 43744, lob logical reads 0, lob physical reads 0, lob
read-ahead reads 0.
Table 'Users'. Scan count 1, logical reads 3696, physical reads 125, read-
ahead reads 0, lob logical reads 0, lob physical reads 0, lob read-ahead
reads 0.

 SQL Server Execution Times:
   CPU time = 59125 ms,  elapsed time = 61267 ms.
 SQL Server Execution Times:
   CPU time = 59125 ms,  elapsed time = 61267 ms.
```

While working through this rewrite, I tried a CROSS APPLY for both the Posts table
and the Votes table, but the performance was almost as bad as the original query.
I decided to try the joins and the GROUP BY clause after that and got Wthe improved
performance that we were looking for. Although we can talk about general best practices,
a good thing to remember is that nothing works great in all situations. Trying as many
scenarios as possible will help you squeeze the most performance out of code.

Summary

Rules of thumb that will really help when rewriting code are the following:

1. Document code thoroughly to help target problem areas to rewrite.

2. Get rid of loops and cursors if possible.

3. Minimize the number of calls to any table.

4. Be aware of how your application uses tempdb before you add
    more temporary structures.

5. Try a few ways of rewriting code to see which works best in each
    situation.

Good job so far! We've made some performance headway on this code. Let's see
what other sneaky gremlins are lying in wait for us in this database code.

CHAPTER 7

Functions

Functions can come in a couple of flavors. There are table-valued functions, in which you can pass in one or a group of values and get a table of values in return. There are also scalar-valued functions, in which you pass in one or a group of values and get a single return value.

Aggregate functions are functions that operate on a group of values to return a single value. There are several built-in functions of SQL Server that perform aggregation: COUNT(), MIN(), MAX(), SUM(), and others. All of these, with the exception of COUNT(), ignore NULL values. You may also create your own user-defined aggregate function, but you need to use CLR assemblies, and that is beyond the scope of this book.

Depending on where functions are used in your code, they can be a large source of performance problems. Almost all performance problems will come from scalar-valued functions; table-valued functions work on a set by definition and are usually used in a more benign way than scalar-valued functions.

Scalar Functions

Let's look at a simple example. Say we have a function to increment a number by one. (Don't laugh – I have seen this in the wild. Yes, really.) The function's alter statement is shown in Listing 7-1.

Listing 7-1. Alter statement for the scalar-valued function dbo.increment

```
ALTER FUNCTION dbo.increment (@someint int)
RETURNS int
AS
BEGIN
RETURN(@someint + 1);
END;
GO
```

© Lisa Bohm 2020
L. Bohm, *Refactoring Legacy T-SQL for Improved Performance*, https://doi.org/10.1007/978-1-4842-5581-0_7

We're going to run a query to demonstrate using the function. The first query we'll run is shown in Listing 7-2. For now, we're going to leave the function call commented out in this query to get baseline data without the use of the function. Also, please turn STATISTICS IO and TIME on before running the query.

Listing 7-2. Simple query to list posts with a score of 320

```
SELECT p.Id
      , p.Score
--      , dbo.increment(p.Score) AS oneAdded
FROM dbo.Posts p
WHERE p.Score = 320;
```

Our STATISTICS IO/TIME output from the query in Listing 7-2 is as follows:

```
(62 rows affected)
Table 'Posts'. Scan count 1, logical reads 3, physical reads 0, read-ahead
reads 0, lob logical reads 0, lob physical reads 0, lob read-ahead reads 0.
 SQL Server Execution Times:
   CPU time = 0 ms,  elapsed time = 0 ms.
SQL Server parse and compile time:
   CPU time = 0 ms, elapsed time = 0 ms.
 SQL Server Execution Times:
   CPU time = 0 ms,  elapsed time = 0 ms.
```

Not a whole lot is going on in this query, which is to be expected. It's a very simple query, and the WHERE clause is based on a column that is indexed. When we add the function line in by uncommenting it, our STATISTICS IO/TIME output doesn't change at all:

```
(62 rows affected)
Table 'Posts'. Scan count 1, logical reads 3, physical reads 0, read-ahead
reads 0, lob logical reads 0, lob physical reads 0, lob read-ahead reads 0.
 SQL Server Execution Times:
   CPU time = 0 ms,  elapsed time = 0 ms.
SQL Server parse and compile time:
   CPU time = 0 ms, elapsed time = 0 ms.
 SQL Server Execution Times:
   CPU time = 0 ms,  elapsed time = 0 ms.
```

Viewing STATISTICS IO Caused by Functions

That doesn't make any sense! Now, one thing I want to caution you here on: STATISTICS IO does NOT show the I/O of functions. We briefly mentioned that earlier in the book, but it's worth restating. For that, we'd need to use an Extended Event. We could use a Profiler trace, but that is pretty outdated. Also note please that Extended Event duration time is natively measured in microseconds, not milliseconds.

If you have run the database setup script for this book, the Event Session should already exist in your database. If not, Listing 7-3 shows how to create the session we're going to use.

Listing 7-3. Create script for an Event Session IO Patterns

```
CREATE EVENT SESSION [IO Patterns] ON SERVER
ADD EVENT sqlserver.sp_statement_completed(
ACTION(sqlserver.sql_text,sqlserver.tsql_stack)),
ADD EVENT sqlserver.sql_statement_completed(
ACTION(sqlserver.sql_text,sqlserver.tsql_stack))
ADD TARGET package0.event_file(SET filename=N'C:\SSdata\IOPatterns.xel');
```

You'll need to change the file target to a directory that exists on your server or computer, wherever you're running SQL Server. To start the session, use the code in Listing 7-4. Go ahead and start the session now.

Listing 7-4. Start the Event Session

```
ALTER EVENT SESSION [IO Patterns] ON SERVER
STATE = START;
GO
```

Let's go back and rerun both the query in Listing 7-2 with the function line commented out and the same query with the function line not commented out. First, we'll run the query with the function commented out. So start the session, run the query, and then stop the session using the code in Listing 7-5.

Listing 7-5. Stop the Event Session

```
ALTER EVENT SESSION [IO Patterns] ON SERVER
STATE = STOP;
GO
```

Extended Event data is saved as XML. In order to view it, we can use SQL Server's XML parsing ability along with an internal function which will allow us to read the Extended Event file. We can use the code in Listing 7-6 to look at the results of the session we started with Listing 7-4. Please be sure to change the file path to match the correct file path in your environment.

Listing 7-6. Code to review the Extended Event session data

```
SELECT
  event_data_XML.value ('(/event/data   [@name="duration"       ]/value)[1]',
  'BIGINT'            ) AS duration,
  event_data_XML.value ('(/event/data   [@name="cpu time"       ]/value)[1]',
  'BIGINT'          ) AS cpu time,
  event_data_XML.value ('(/event/data   [@name="physical reads"]/value)[1]',
  'BIGINT'          ) AS physical reads,
  event_data_XML.value ('(/event/data   [@name="logical reads" ]/value)[1]',
  'BIGINT'          ) AS logical reads,
  event_data_XML.value ('(/event/data   [@name="writes"        ]/value)[1]',
  'BIGINT'          ) AS writes,
  event_data_XML.value ('(/event/data   [@name="row count"     ]/value)[1]',
  'BIGINT'          ) AS row count,
  event_data_XML.value ('(/event/data   [@name="statement"     ]/value)[1]',
  'NVARCHAR(4000)') AS [statement]
FROM (SELECT CAST(event_data AS XML) AS event_data_XML
    FROM sys.fn_xe_file_target_read_file('c:\SSdata\IOPatterns*.xel',
    null, null, null) AS F
                ) AS E;
```

When we look at the Event Session file that was generated when we ran the query in Listing 7-2 with the function commented out, we get the result set shown in Table 7-1.

Table 7-1. *Results from Extended Event after running query in Listing 7-2 without function*

duration	cpu time	physical reads	logical reads	writes	row count	statement
190	0	0	3	0	62	SELECT p.Id, p.Score --, dbo.increment(p.Score) AS oneAdded FROM dbo.Posts p WHERE p.Score = 320

The results in Table 7-1 mirror the STATISTICS IO and TIME results for the same query. Remember the `duration` of our Extended Event is in microseconds! What would our Extended Event output look like when we include a function in our query? Let's see, using the following steps:

1. Delete the Extended Event file.

2. Start the Extended Event session using the code in Listing 7-4.

3. Run the query in Listing 7-2, with the function line NOT commented out.

4. Stop the Extended Event session using the code in Listing 7-5.

5. Review the output using the code in Listing 7-6, which we see in Table 7-2.

Table 7-2. *Results from Extended Event after running query in Listing 7-2 with function*

duration	cpu time	physical reads	logical reads	writes	row count	statement
2	0	0	0	0	1	RETURN(@someint + 1)
1	0	0	0	0	1	RETURN(@someint + 1)
1	0	0	0	0	1	RETURN(@someint + 1)
1	0	0	0	0	1	RETURN(@someint + 1)
0	0	0	0	0	1	RETURN(@someint + 1)
0	0	0	0	0	1	RETURN(@someint + 1)
1	0	0	0	0	1	RETURN(@someint + 1)
1	0	0	0	0	1	RETURN(@someint + 1)
0	0	0	0	0	1	RETURN(@someint + 1)
1	0	0	0	0	1	RETURN(@someint + 1)
1	0	0	0	0	1	RETURN(@someint + 1)
1	0	0	0	0	1	RETURN(@someint + 1)
1	0	0	0	0	1	RETURN(@someint + 1)
0	0	0	0	0	1	RETURN(@someint + 1)
0	0	0	0	0	1	RETURN(@someint + 1)
1	0	0	0	0	1	RETURN(@someint + 1)
1	0	0	0	0	1	RETURN(@someint + 1)
1	0	0	0	0	1	RETURN(@someint + 1)
0	0	0	0	0	1	RETURN(@someint + 1)
0	0	0	0	0	1	RETURN(@someint + 1)
1	0	0	0	0	1	RETURN(@someint + 1)
0	0	0	0	0	1	RETURN(@someint + 1)
0	0	0	0	0	1	RETURN(@someint + 1)

(continued)

Table 7-2. (*continued*)

duration	cpu time	physical reads	logical reads	writes	row count	statement
1	0	0	0	0	1	RETURN(@someint + 1)
0	0	0	0	0	1	RETURN(@someint + 1)
1	0	0	0	0	1	RETURN(@someint + 1)
1	0	0	0	0	1	RETURN(@someint + 1)
0	0	0	0	0	1	RETURN(@someint + 1)
1	0	0	0	0	1	RETURN(@someint + 1)
1	0	0	0	0	1	RETURN(@someint + 1)
0	0	0	0	0	1	RETURN(@someint + 1)
0	0	0	0	0	1	RETURN(@someint + 1)
1	0	0	0	0	1	RETURN(@someint + 1)
0	0	0	0	0	1	RETURN(@someint + 1)
1	0	0	0	0	1	RETURN(@someint + 1)
1	0	0	0	0	1	RETURN(@someint + 1)
1	0	0	0	0	1	RETURN(@someint + 1)
0	0	0	0	0	1	RETURN(@someint + 1)
0	0	0	0	0	1	RETURN(@someint + 1)
0	0	0	0	0	1	RETURN(@someint + 1)
0	0	0	0	0	1	RETURN(@someint + 1)
0	0	0	0	0	1	RETURN(@someint + 1)
1	0	0	0	0	1	RETURN(@someint + 1)
0	0	0	0	0	1	RETURN(@someint + 1)
0	0	0	0	0	1	RETURN(@someint + 1)
0	0	0	0	0	1	RETURN(@someint + 1)
1	0	0	0	0	1	RETURN(@someint + 1)

(*continued*)

Table 7-2. (*continued*)

duration	cpu time	physical reads	logical reads	writes	row count	statement
0	0	0	0	0	1	RETURN(@someint + 1)
0	0	0	0	0	1	RETURN(@someint + 1)
0	0	0	0	0	1	RETURN(@someint + 1)
0	0	0	0	0	1	RETURN(@someint + 1)
0	0	0	0	0	1	RETURN(@someint + 1)
0	0	0	0	0	1	RETURN(@someint + 1)
0	0	0	0	0	1	RETURN(@someint + 1)
1	0	0	0	0	1	RETURN(@someint + 1)
1	0	0	0	0	1	RETURN(@someint + 1)
0	0	0	0	0	1	RETURN(@someint + 1)
0	0	0	0	0	1	RETURN(@someint + 1)
1	0	0	0	0	1	RETURN(@someint + 1)
0	0	0	0	0	1	RETURN(@someint + 1)
0	0	0	0	0	1	RETURN(@someint + 1)
1	0	0	0	0	1	RETURN(@someint + 1)
2925	0	0	5	0	124	SELECT p.Id, p.Score, dbo.increment(p.Score) AS oneAdded FROM dbo.Posts p WHERE p.Score = 320

Table 7-2 shows us a very different picture than we saw in Table 7-1, or the original STATISTICS IO and TIME output. We can see a difference in the duration and the logical reads. The Extended Event thinks the row count has doubled. What are all these RETURN statements? They are the function running: once against each row of the output. WHOA! This can add up to a whole lot of extra work. What if this was a much more complicated function? Well, we'll get to that. First, let's look to see what would happen if the function was in the WHERE clause.

Scalar-Valued Functions in a WHERE Clause

I'm going to add additional limits in the test WHERE clause because otherwise we're going to get too much data back in the Extended Event. Let's use the following steps:

1. Delete the Extended Event file.

2. Start the Extended Event session using the code in Listing 7-4.

3. Run the query in Listing 7-7.

4. Stop the Extended Event session using the code in Listing 7-5.

5. Review the output using the code in Listing 7-6, which we see in Table 7-2.

Listing 7-7. Query with a function in the WHERE clause

```
SELECT p.Id
    , p.Score
FROM dbo.Posts p
WHERE p.Score > 315
    AND p.Score < 325
    AND dbo.increment(p.Score) = 321;
```

You'll likely see functions in the WHERE clause in the wild more often as "I want to see what happened yesterday," so the function will add a day to a column and see if it equals today, for example. This query took 9 minutes to run! What is going on here? If we look at our Extended Event output, we see **629 rows** like the first row of Table 7-3 and a single row at the end with the full query.

Table 7-3. *Results from Extended Event showing data from query in Listing 7-7*

duration	cpu time	physical reads	logical reads	writes	row count	Statement	NumRows
1	0	0	0	0	1	RETURN (@someint + 1)	629
24790	15000	0	6	0	691	SELECT p.Id, p.Score FROM dbo. Posts p WHERE p.Score > 315 AND p.Score < 325 AND dbo.increment (p.Score) = 321	1

The result set of the query in Listing 7-7 only shows 62 rows returned. Why is the function running 629 times? We're asking in this query to find when the increment of the score equals the number we specified. The only way SQL Server can determine if the increment of the score is equivalent another value is to first determine the increment of every (yes, every) record in the Posts table. In this case, we limited the values to the number of posts that have a score between 315 and 325, which is why the function ran only 629 times; there are only 629 posts with a score between 315 and 325. This is a lot of work that we're now asking the server to do.

In most cases, instead of using the function against the table column, we should use the function against a parameter. We can then have the benefit of having a possibly complex calculation set up so we can reuse it, but will not pay the penalty of having this run against every record in the table!

Native SQL Server Functions

In the case of "I want to see what happened yesterday," instead of using the function against the table column, we should use the function against the parameter. We can see even native SQL Server functions like DATEADD(), ISNULL(), and COALESCE() causing the query to have to evaluate every record in a table. Let's use the code in Listing 7-8 to see the difference this can make.

Listing 7-8. Sample query with a date function in the WHERE clause

```
DECLARE @date date;
SET @date='20120801';

SELECT p.Id
    , p.Score
FROM dbo.Posts p
WHERE DATEADD(dd,1,CAST(p.CreationDate AS date)) = @date;
```

What kind of data are we expecting from this query? For example, how many posts were created on the date in question? If we're looking at adding one day to the date after stripping out the time and that value being equal to 2012.08.01, then we're talking about all posts that were created between 2012.07.31 and 2012.08.01. First, let's use the code in Listing 7-9 to see how many posts we are expecting.

Listing 7-9. Number of posts expected in the result set of the query in Listing 7-8

```
SELECT COUNT(1) AS numPosts
    , CAST(p.CreationDate AS date) AS theDay
FROM dbo.Posts p
WHERE p.CreationDate > '20120731'
AND p.CreationDate < '20120801'
GROUP BY CAST(p.CreationDate AS date)
ORDER BY theDay;
```

The results from the query in Listing 7-9 are shown in Table 7-4. What these results mean is that we'd expect 16,154 rows of output when we run our query from Listing 7-8.

Table 7-4. *Results from running the query in Listing 7-9*

numPosts	theDay
16154	2012-07-31

If we turn on our Event Session and run the query from Listing 7-8, we first of all see the 16,154 records that we expect to see. We don't see the "extra" lines in the Extended Event session output (shown in Table 7-5), but we do see a significant amount of logical reads. So how would we rewrite the code from Listing 7-8 to remove the native SQL Server function from the query?

Table 7-5. Extended Event session results from running the query in Listing 7-8

duration	cpu time	physical reads	logical reads	writes	row count	statement
6307209	6297000	0	111,345	0	16154	SELECT p.Id, p.Score FROM dbo.Posts p WHERE DATEADD(dd,1,CAST (p.CreationDate AS date)) = @date

First, we need to create begin and end dates, and use those to find a range of creationdates, or any dates between those times. Your end date will become the date you pass in, because according to the code, you want all posts that were created in the day before the date we passed in. By using the DATEADD() function against the parameter, we can move it out of the query itself, as shown in Listing 7-10.

Listing 7-10. Moving DATEADD() function to the parameter and out of the query

```
DECLARE @date date
, @startdate date;
SET @date='20120801';
SET @startdate = DATEADD(dd,-1,@date);

SELECT p.Id
     , p.Score
FROM dbo.Posts p
WHERE p.CreationDate >= @startdate
     AND p.CreationDate < @date;
```

Let's go back and clean up by deleting the Extended Event file and restarting our Event Session. Then, run the code in Listing 7-10. We still get the 16,154 rows returned that we expected, but the Extended Event session data in Table 7-6 shows a reduction in the work the server is doing.

Table 7-6. *Extended Event session results from running the query in Listing 7-10*

duration	cpu time	physical reads	logical reads	writes	row count	statement
5593747	5578000	0	29,771	0	16154	SELECT p.Id, p.Score FROM dbo.Posts p WHERE p.CreationDate >= @startdate AND p.CreationDate < @date

In Table 7-6, we see that removing the DATEADD() function from the query in Listing 7-8 decreases the time by almost a second, and the logical reads have been reduced from over 100,000 to about 30,000. Now we know be very, very careful using functions, especially any sort of scalar-valued function in a WHERE clause!

The Dreaded "Massive Business Logic" Function

We have looked at a very simple function and a native SQL Server function. I want to point you toward a couple of other things to be aware of. First of all, there's the "massive business logic" function – a several-thousand-line function that does a whole bunch of things. When you come across these, break them up and try to use them in-line in stored procedures when you can. The sp_codeCalledCascade can help here so you can at least identify any SQL objects calling these behemoths.

One flavor of these are the "kitchen sink" functions. I'm going to pass in an ID-type value (post ID perhaps) and what I want to get back (a tag of some sort), and the function will then return that value. Let's look at the example function in Listing 7-11.

Listing 7-11. Alter statement for the andTheKitchenSink function

```
ALTER FUNCTION dbo.andTheKitchenSink (@postID int, @value varchar(8))
RETURNS varchar(30)
AS
BEGIN
DECLARE @returnValue varchar(30)
, @numComments varchar(30)
, @numResponses varchar(30)
, @numResponders varchar(30)
, @numLinks varchar(30)
, @numVotes varchar(30)
;

SET @numComments = COALESCE((SELECT CAST(COUNT(1) AS varchar(30))
                            FROM dbo.Comments
                            WHERE PostId = @postID),'0');
SET @numResponses = COALESCE((SELECT CAST(COUNT(1) AS varchar(30))
                            FROM dbo.Posts
                            WHERE ParentId = @postID
                                AND PostTypeId = 2),'0');
SET @numResponders = COALESCE((SELECT CAST(COUNT(DISTINCT OwnerUserID) AS
varchar(30))
                            FROM dbo.Posts
                            WHERE ParentId = @postID
                                AND PostTypeId = 2),'0');
SET @numLinks = COALESCE((SELECT CAST(COUNT(1) AS varchar(30))
                            FROM dbo.PostLinks
                            WHERE PostId = @postID),'0');
SET @numVotes = COALESCE((SELECT CAST(COUNT(1) AS varchar(30))
                            FROM dbo.Votes
                            WHERE PostId = @postID),'0');
SET @returnValue = CASE @value
                        WHEN 'COMMENT' THEN @numComments
                        WHEN 'RESPDR' THEN @numResponders
                        WHEN 'LINK' THEN @numLinks
```

```
                          WHEN 'VOTE' THEN @numVotes
                          ELSE @numResponses
                          END;
RETURN(@returnValue);
END;
GO
```

What's the first concerning thing you notice about this? Oh – you, there in the back – you have your hand raised. That's right! Even though we're only returning a single value, we're actually doing the work to get all of the values every time this is called! No one would really do that, right? Wrong. I have actually come across this type of function (but worse, with about 30 values) more than once in the wild. These can be called several times in a single SELECT statement. It will go out, hit the tables called, and get every value in the function every time it shows up in the SELECT statement, for every row. That is really frightening, and downright damaging to the SQL Server's performance. It is not noticeable when there's only a little data in the database, but it sure becomes obvious as data grows over time. Let's reset our Extended Event session and run the code in Listing 7-12.

Listing 7-12. Sample query using the andTheKitchenSink function

```
SELECT p.id AS postID
     , p.Score
     , dbo.andTheKitchenSink(649789,'COMMENT') AS numComments
     , dbo.andTheKitchenSink(649789,'RESPONS') AS numResponses
     , dbo.andTheKitchenSink(649789,'RESPDR') AS numResponders
     , dbo.andTheKitchenSink(649789,'VOTE') AS numVotes
     , p.ViewCount
FROM dbo.Posts p
WHERE p.Id = 649789;
```

We get a single row returned as the results from the query, which is expected. When we look at the Extended Event session output shown in Table 7-7, we get an idea of all of the work going on in the background to return that single row. I truncated the statement to make the table much more readable.

Table 7-7. *Extended Event session output from running the query in Listing 7-12, with the statement truncated*

duration	cpu time	physical reads	logical reads	writes	row count	statement
367	0	0	262	0	1	SET @numResponses = ...
99	0	0	6	0	1	SET @numComments = ...
1	0	0	0	0	1	RETURN(@returnValue)
126	0	0	6	0	1	SET @numVotes = ...
2	0	0	0	0	1	SET @returnValue = ...
561	0	0	262	0	1	SET @numResponders = ...
59	0	0	6	0	1	SET @numComments = ...
61	0	0	6	0	1	SET @numLinks = ...
449	0	0	262	0	1	SET @numResponses = ...
532	0	0	262	0	1	SET @numResponders = ...
1	0	0	0	0	1	SET @returnValue = ...
1	0	0	0	0	1	RETURN(@returnValue)
130	15000	0	6	0	1	SET @numComments = ...
132	0	0	6	0	1	SET @numVotes = ...
351	0	0	262	0	1	SET @numResponses = ...
88	0	0	6	0	1	SET @numLinks = ...
1	0	0	0	0	1	SET @returnValue = ...
1	0	0	0	0	1	RETURN(@returnValue)
124	0	0	6	0	1	SET @numVotes = ...
559	0	0	262	0	1	SET @numResponders = ...
57	0	0	6	0	1	SET @numLinks = ...
70	0	0	6	0	1	SET @numComments = ...
127	0	0	6	0	1	SET @numLinks = ...

(continued)

Table 7-7. (*continued*)

duration	cpu time	physical reads	logical reads	writes	row count	statement
310	0	0	262	0	1	SET @numResponses = ...
415	0	0	262	0	1	SET @numResponders = ...
1	0	0	0	0	1	RETURN(@returnValue)
165	0	0	6	0	1	SET @numVotes = ...
4	0	0	0	0	1	SET @returnValue = ...
6211	15000	0	2174	0	29	SELECT p.Id AS postID, p.Score, dbo.andTheKitchenSink (p.id,'COMMENT') AS numComments, dbo.andTheKitchenSink (p.id,'RESPONS') AS numResponses, dbo.andTheKitchenSink (p.id,'RESPDR') AS numResponders, dbo.andTheKitchenSink (p.id,'VOTE') AS numVotes, p.ViewCount FROM dbo.Posts p WHERE p.Id = 649789

We can see by the data in Table 7-7 that all of the pieces of data in the andTheKitchenSink function were found for each of the calls in the query (there were four), and this would show for each record in the final output as well if we were returning more than one row.

Imagine trying to wade through this Extended Event output if we were returning several rows! If we want to look at some totals metrics instead of each individual record, we can use the query shown in listing 7-13.

Listing 7-13. Viewing totals metrics for Extended Event session data

```
SELECT SUM(duration)/1000 AS totDurationms
, SUM(cpu time)/1000 AS totCPUms
, SUM(logical reads) AS totLogReads
FROM(
SELECT
  event_data_XML.value ('(/event/data  [@name="duration"    ]/value)[1]',
  'BIGINT'      ) AS duration,
  event_data_XML.value ('(/event/data  [@name="cpu time"     ]/value)[1]',
  'BIGINT'       ) AS cpu time,
  event_data_XML.value ('(/event/data  [@name="physical reads"]/value)[1]',
  'BIGINT'        ) AS physical reads,
  event_data_XML.value ('(/event/data  [@name="logical reads" ]/value)[1]',
  'BIGINT'        ) AS logical reads,
  event_data_XML.value ('(/event/data  [@name="writes"        ]/value)[1]',
  'BIGINT'       ) AS writes,
  event_data_XML.value ('(/event/data  [@name="row count"     ]/value)[1]',
  'BIGINT'       ) AS row count,
  event_data_XML.value ('(/event/data  [@name="statement"     ]/value)[1]',
  'NVARCHAR(4000)') AS [statement]
FROM (SELECT CAST(event_data AS XML) AS event_data_XML
                FROM sys.fn_xe_file_target_read_file('c:\SSdata\
                IOPatterns*.xel', null, null, null) AS F
                ) AS E) q;
```

If we run this query against the file whose results we were looking at in Table 7-7, we would get a much better idea of the actual work the server is doing, as shown in Table 7-8.

Table 7-8. Totals metrics for Extended
Event session data in Table 7-7

totDurationms	totCPUms	totLogReads
11	30	4,346

Even though this query isn't particularly painful when returning one record, it could become very painful if used to return a larger set. Besides, why make SQL Server do more work than it needs to? Use those powers for good, not evil! Let's look at rewriting the andTheKitchenSink function to minimize the work we're doing, and only perform the work we need to do to find the value we want. How do we do this? One way is to only run the code to find the value if the corresponding @value tag is passed in. We can do this by setting the @returnValue using a CASE statement and basing the query run to get the @returnValue on the value of the @value tag. We've done this in the code in Listing 7-14.

Listing 7-14. Rewrite of andTheKitchenSink to only get the desired value

```
ALTER FUNCTION dbo.andTheKitchenSink (@postID int, @value varchar(8))
RETURNS varchar(30)
AS
BEGIN
DECLARE @returnValue varchar(30);
SET @returnValue = CASE @value
                WHEN 'COMMENT' THEN COALESCE((SELECT CAST(COUNT(1) AS
                varchar(30))
                        FROM dbo.Comments
                        WHERE PostId = @postID),'0')
                WHEN 'RESPDR' THEN COALESCE((SELECT CAST(COUNT(DISTINCT
                OwnerUserID) AS varchar(30))
                        FROM dbo.Posts
                        WHERE ParentId = @postID
                            AND PostTypeId = 2),'0')
            WHEN 'LINK' THEN COALESCE((SELECT CAST(COUNT(1) AS varchar(30))
                        FROM dbo.PostLinks
                        WHERE PostId = @postID),'0')
                WHEN 'VOTE' THEN COALESCE((SELECT CAST(COUNT(1) AS
                varchar(30))
                        FROM dbo.Votes
                        WHERE PostId = @postID),'0')
                ELSE COALESCE((SELECT CAST(COUNT(1) AS varchar(30))
                        FROM dbo.Posts
                        WHERE ParentId = @postID
```

```
                                    AND PostTypeId = 2),'0')
                END;

RETURN(@returnValue);
END;
GO
```

Let's use the code in Listing 7-14 to update our andTheKitchenSink function and then reset our Extended Event session. Run the query in Listing 7-12 again, and we'll look at the Extended Event output in Table 7-9 using the code in Listing 7-6.

Table 7-9. *Extended Event session output from running the query in Listing 7-12 against the updated andTheKitchenSink function*

Duration	cpu time	physical reads	logical reads	Writes	row count	Statement
1	0	0	0	0	1	RETURN(@returnValue)
278	0	0	6	0	1	SET @returnValue = ...
1	0	0	0	0	1	RETURN(@returnValue)
1	0	0	0	0	1	RETURN(@returnValue)
549	16000	0	262	0	1	SET @returnValue = ...
560	0	0	262	0	1	SET @returnValue = ...
1	0	0	0	0	1	RETURN(@returnValue)
343	0	0	6	0	1	SET @returnValue = ...
2213	16000	0	542	0	9	SELECT p.Id AS postID, p.Score, dbo.andTheKitchenSink(p.id, 'COMMENT') AS numComments, dbo.andTheKitchenSink(p.id, 'RESPONS') AS numResponses, dbo.andTheKitchenSink(p.id, 'RESPDR') AS numResponders, dbo.andTheKitchenSink(p.id,'VOTE') AS numVotes, p.ViewCount FROM dbo.Posts p WHERE p.Id = 649789

We can clearly see in Table 7-9 that our CASE statement was called four times, instead of the 20 different queries called in Table 7-7. We'll run the code from Listing 7-13 against our Extended Event session file to view our totals, which are shown in Table 7-10.

Table 7-10. *Totals metrics for Extended*
Event session data in Table 7-9

totDurationms	totCPUms	totLogReads
4	32	1,082

Getting rid of the extra work really makes a huge difference in terms of duration and total logical reads! At this point, would I rewrite the query in Listing 7-12 to pull the functionality out of the function and in-line it with the query? Probably not, if we were always returning just a single record. Also, if each of the pieces of data found through the andTheKitchenSink function were calling the same database table, I probably would rewrite the query. But most of the data comes from different tables.

Using OUTER APPLY to Join Aggregate Data

Additionally, if there were more than one row in the output, I would also move the code which finds our additional data to joins or OUTER APPLYs. What would that look like? We can look at the code in Listing 7-15 to see a method using OUTER APPLY. For pieces of data that come from the same table, we can combine the metrics in the same OUTER APPLY.

Listing 7-15. Using OUTER APPLY to find additional aggregate data

```
SELECT p.Id AS postID
    , p.Score
    , com.numComments
    , resp.numResponses
    , resp.numResponders
    , vote.numVotes
    , p.ViewCount
FROM dbo.Posts p
```

```
OUTER APPLY (SELECT COUNT(1) AS numComments
            FROM dbo.Comments c
            WHERE c.PostId = p.Id) com
OUTER APPLY (SELECT COUNT(DISTINCT OwnerUserID) AS numResponders
                  , COUNT(Id) AS numResponses
            FROM dbo.Posts resp
            WHERE resp.PostTypeId = 2
                  AND p.Id = resp.ParentId) resp
OUTER APPLY (SELECT COUNT(1) AS numVotes
            FROM dbo.Votes v
            WHERE v.PostId = p.Id) vote
WHERE p.Id = 649789;
```

If we reset our Extended Event session, we can run the query in Listing 7-15 to see if this is going to make a difference on our query run metrics. The data from the Extended Event session is shown in Table 7-11.

Table 7-11. *Extended Event session output from running the query in Listing 7-15*

duration	cpu time	physical reads	logical reads	writes	row count	statement
576	0	0	149	0	1	SELECT p.Id AS postID, p.Score, com. numComments, respInfo.numResponses, respInfo.numResponders, vote.numVotes, p.ViewCount FROM dbo.Posts p OUTER APPLY (SELECT COUNT(1) AS numComments FROM dbo.Comments c WHERE c.PostId = p.Id) com OUTER APPLY (SELECT COUNT(DISTINCT resp.OwnerUserID) AS numResponders, COUNT(resp.Id) AS numResponses FROM dbo. Posts resp WHERE resp.PostTypeId = 2 AND p.Id = resp.ParentId) respInfo OUTER APPLY (SELECT COUNT(1) AS numVotes FROM dbo. Votes v WHERE v.PostId = p.Id) vote WHERE p.Id = 649789

Remember duration here is in microseconds, as opposed to our totals query, where we changed the duration to be in milliseconds. The query in Listing 7-15 ran in about half a millisecond and only used one-tenth of the reads. What would the difference be with a query returning many post IDs? Remember we're now using the "new" rewritten kitchen sink function from Listing 7-14. The code in Listing 7-16 will update our query to return several rows instead of a single row.

Metrics with Increasing Number of Return Rows

Listing 7-16. Query calling the andTheKitchenSink function, returning several rows

```
SELECT p.Id AS postID
     , p.Score
     , dbo.andTheKitchenSink(649789,'COMMENT') AS numComments
     , dbo.andTheKitchenSink(649789,'RESPONS') AS numResponses
     , dbo.andTheKitchenSink(649789,'RESPDR') AS numResponders
     , dbo.andTheKitchenSink(649789,'VOTE') AS numVotes
     , p.ViewCount
FROM dbo.Posts p
WHERE p.Score = 320;
```

We already know from earlier in the book that this will output 62 rows, and we can see if we look at the Extended Event session totals, shown in Table 7-12, that the code still runs in less than a second.

Table 7-12. *Totals metrics for Extended Event session for code in Listing 7-16*

totDurationms	totCPUms	totLogReads
160	157	7,073

Next, let's reset our Extended Event session. We should try the query version using the OUTER APPLY code instead of the andTheKitchenSink function, shown in Listing 7-17. Then, we can see if our metrics differ with more rows of output.

Listing 7-17. Using OUTER APPLY to find additional aggregate data, against multiple rows

```
SELECT p.Id AS postID
         , p.Score
         , com.numComments
         , respInfo.numResponses
         , respInfo.numResponders
         , vote.numVotes
         , p.ViewCount
FROM dbo.Posts p
OUTER APPLY (SELECT COUNT(1) AS numComments
               FROM dbo.Comments c
               WHERE c.PostId = p.Id) com
OUTER APPLY (SELECT COUNT(DISTINCT resp.OwnerUserID) AS numResponders
               , COUNT(resp.Id) AS numResponses
            FROM dbo.Posts resp
            WHERE resp.PostTypeId = 2
               AND p.Id = resp.ParentId) respInfo
OUTER APPLY (SELECT COUNT(1) AS numVotes
               FROM dbo.Votes v
               WHERE v.PostId = p.Id) vote
WHERE p.score = 320;
```

When we run the code from Listing 7-13 against our Extended Event session file, we get the totals metrics shown in Table 7-13. We show significant improvement in metrics with the additional information-gathering code in-line in the query, as opposed to calling the scalar-valued function. The improvement is much more significant as the return records increase in number.

Table 7-13. *Totals metrics for Extended Event session for code in Listing 7-17*

totDurationms	totCPUms	totLogReads
7	16	1,529

Is there ever a place for a scalar-valued function? Perhaps. I generally do not use them, but I can see where they could be useful. Say every night I run a procedure that gives a bonus to people who respond depending on what day of the week it is, or whether it's a holiday. The calculation to determine whether it's a holiday, weekend, or workday may be somewhat complicated. I could see writing a function to pass in a date and have it determine which type of day it is and therefore what the multiplier for the bonus would be. I can call the function at the beginning of my procedure, save the return value in a variable, and use it to calculate the correct bonus for each person responding to a question that day.

Table Valued Functions (TVFs)

There are two different types of table-valued functions: in-line TVFs and multi-statement TVFs. The syntax is a bit different, and you can only have a single select statement in an in-line TVF. You may have more complex logic in a multi-statement TVF, but you will also get a corresponding performance hit. Even an in-line TVF and a multi-statement TVF doing the "same work" will result in the in-line TVF performing much better. Let's take a look at the multi-statement TVF in Listing 7-18.

Listing 7-18. Alter statement from responderInfoMultiValue

```
ALTER FUNCTION dbo.responderInfoMultiValue (@postID int)
RETURNS @userInfo TABLE
          (DisplayName nvarchar(40)
               , Reputation int
               , WebsiteURL nvarchar(200)
          )
AS
BEGIN
DECLARE @userList TABLE (ownerUserID int);

INSERT INTO @userList (ownerUserID)
SELECT p.OwnerUserId
FROM dbo.Posts p
WHERE p.ParentId = @postID
     AND p.PostTypeId = 2;
```

```
 INSERT INTO @userInfo (DisplayName, Reputation, WebsiteURL)
 SELECT u.DisplayName
             , u.Reputation
             , u.WebsiteUrl
FROM dbo.Users u
INNER JOIN @userlist ul ON ul.OwnerUserId = u.Id;
RETURN
END;
GO
```

Let's go back and reset our Extended Event session. Then, we can run the code in Listing 7-19 to look at some metrics around running code calling the multi-statement TVF in Listing 7-18.

Listing 7-19. Query calling the responderInfoMultiValue function

```
SELECT DisplayName
      , Reputation
FROM dbo.responderInfoMultiValue(649789); --the number is a post ID
```

When we run the code in Listing 7-19, our query returns 31 records. If we take a look at our Extended Event session data using the code in Listing 7-6, we get the results shown in Table 7-14.

Table 7-14. *Extended Event session output from running the query in Listing 7-19*

duration	cpu time	physical reads	logical reads	writes	row count	statement
522	0	0	164	0	32	INSERT INTO @userList (OwnerUserId) SELECT p.OwnerUserId FROM dbo.Posts p WHERE p.ParentId = @postID AND p.PostTypeId = 2
712	0	0	131	0	31	INSERT INTO @userInfo (DisplayName, Reputation, WebsiteURL) SELECT u.DisplayName, u.Reputation, u.WebsiteUrl FROM dbo.Users u INNER JOIN @userlist ul ON ul.OwnerUserId = u.Id
1796	0	0	310	0	94	SELECT DisplayName, Reputation FROM dbo. responderInfoMultiValue(649789)

Alternatively, the code can be written as an in-line TVF. The syntax is a little different, as shown by the statement RETURNS TABLE instead of defining the entire table structure to be returned. Additionally, note that there is only a single SELECT statement in the code in Listing 7-20.

Listing 7-20. Alter statement for the responderInfoInline function

```
ALTER FUNCTION dbo.responderInfoInline (@postID int)
RETURNS TABLE
AS
RETURN SELECT u.DisplayName
            , u.Reputation
            , u.WebsiteUrl
        FROM dbo.Users u
        WHERE EXISTS (SELECT 1
                        FROM dbo.Posts p
                        WHERE p.ParentId = @postID
                          AND u.Id = p.OwnerUserId
                          AND p.PostTypeId = 2);
GO
```

If we run the code in Listing 7-19 but call the in-line version of the function instead, and using the same post ID we did before, we get the same 31 rows, but our Extended Event output looks a bit different, as shown in Table 7-15.

Table 7-15. *Extended Event session output from running the query in Listing 7-19, but against the in-line function*

duration	cpu time	physical reads	logical reads	writes	row count	statement
1621	0	0	227	0	31	SELECT DisplayName, Reputation FROM dbo.responderInfoInline (649789)

That's it – just that one line, with no other work. SQL Server actually in-lines (or translates the function into part of the original query) the code in the function. We see a shorter time and less physical reads using the in-line version of the function over using the multi-statement TVF.

If you're going to do the work anyway to take a multi-statement TVF to an in-line TVF, there's most likely no reason you can't just in-line the code in the stored procedure (or whatever object you're looking at) and remove the function altogether.

Summary

Functions are really a way to reuse code (like the kitchen sink function). As great as code reuse is in front-end programming, it is almost always a bad idea in SQL Server. Write your code for the work you need, and just the work you need. Also, pull your business logic out of the work SQL Server is doing – but that is another discussion for another time, and someone else's book!

PART IV

The Bad and the Ugly

CHAPTER 8

Agent Jobs

SQL Server Agent allows you to set up a schedule to run code at the times you choose. This can be extremely helpful, but can also lead to a very tangled mess. How many times have you heard about periodic slowness in the application or database, but it's always gone by the time you get online to look for it? You need to determine if there is a real pattern to the slowness, then you can see if there are jobs that coincide with the painful times.

First, let's look at what the SQL Server Agent should be accomplishing for you. This first section is a bit more administrative than development, but it is so important that everyone who works with databases should be aware of these needs! Then, we can take a look at how these jobs may be sneaking into your performance problems... or nightmares!

What Agent Jobs Should Be Doing

There are some administrative duties that should be set up as Agent jobs and run either nightly or weekly. These are important to the maintenance and integrity of your database and also to your Disaster Recovery (DR) plan. You DO have one of those at your company, don't you? And you do practice that plan and any associated rollovers, right? Sorry, got distracted for a second. Back to SQL Server Agent!

Good Job(s)!

The "good" jobs should run against every database, including your system databases. Please note that these recommendations are based on databases in the 0–500 GB range. Larger databases may require different strategies.

© Lisa Bohm 2020

L. Bohm, *Refactoring Legacy T-SQL for Improved Performance*, https://doi.org/10.1007/978-1-4842-5581-0_8

1. Full backups: These should be run, at minimum, once every 24 hours. They may need to be run more often, depending on the business and its needs. Larger databases may run full backups less often.

2. Transaction log backups: These should be run, at minimum, once an hour. Again, this depends on the business needs and the loads on the server, but this is a good recommendation to start with.

3. Differential backups: These can be run if needed, based on the business needs and the loads on the servers. I consider these "optional," but the other two backup types mandatory. These may become mandatory if your database is very large and nightly full backups aren't a viable solution.

4. Corruption checks (or DBCC CHECKDB()): This should be run weekly at minimum, but ideally once every 24 hours.

5. Index and statistics maintenance: This should be run also weekly at a minimum, but again it's ideal to run once every 24 hours.

6. Purge jobs: Trim out excess audit or even operational data if not needed.

As with anything related to databases, you must know your environment and software and the usage patterns. Some of the "good" jobs may not be needed in a specific environment, but probably most or all of them should be used. This brings us to the next, and probably the most key, point.

When Should I Run Jobs?

How do you know when backups should be run? How about index maintenance? How about that massive daily report that every manager needs or else the world will come to an end?

Also, it would make sense to run certain jobs before other jobs. For example, it's best to run a corruption check and index maintenance before your nightly full backup. If you ever need to restore to that backup, you have some confidence that it is probably corruption-free and has up-to-date index maintenance, so it is ready to go. This could save you valuable time in getting your environment back online in case of an emergency. The only way to be 100% sure your backup is viable, however, is to test your backups. Ideally, you're also restoring your backups to test them, and this could also be automated with a job.

Understand Your Environment... on a Regular Basis

It is necessary to understand some metrics surrounding your environment to best schedule the Agent jobs. What times during the day show the least CPU usage? What times are the least number of users accessing the system? When is tempdb the least busy? How about when there are the lowest disk writes? If you have a third-party monitoring solution, this information can be simple to find. If not, though, you can still find the information by using a home-grown solution to find this data. There are plenty of blog posts and presentations out in the wild that discuss baselining your servers, whether it's through PowerShell, Extended Events, some mix of the two, or many other solutions as well.

Why does the heading mention "on a regular basis," though? Well, as data grows and possible usage patterns change, the baselines and slow times of your servers will change as well. Jobs that formerly were benign can suddenly cause serious performance problems with a shift of database usage patterns. Additionally, there can be jobs that only come into play once in a while. For example, month-end, quarterly, and year-end reports are run infrequently enough that a pattern of issues may not become evident, but can still plague users.

Understand Your Jobs and the Needs Behind Them... on a Regular Basis

When are your jobs scheduled for? How long do they run? How often do they run? What business need is the job actually answering? For example, you have a customer that needs to have up-to-the-moment summaries of their orders for each day. There is a job that calls a stored procedure that can grab and summarize this data, and it runs every 2 minutes.

Part of the problem is that this proc is starting to take longer than 2 minutes to run, so essentially it is running all of the time. Also, it's pulling and aggregating data by day since the beginning of time, and to the end of time (at least according to database standards). Also, this customer's business is only open from the hours of 9:00 a.m. until 5:00 p.m. and is closed Wednesdays and Sundays.

A few simple changes you can make are to bump the job out to run every 5 minutes, limit the runtimes to start at 9:00 a.m. and end at 5:00 p.m. daily, and also set them not to run on Wednesdays and Sundays.

Again, as time (and data amounts) changes, the jobs that used to be quick may suddenly not run as quickly. For example, your corruption check job may suddenly be running for hours. If this occurs, then maybe a different plan may be best:

1. Run index maintenance.

2. Run your full backup.

3. Send the full backup to your test server (or a read-only reporting secondary).

4. Restore the database.

5. Run your corruption check on your test or secondary environment.

Common Issues with Agent Jobs

We spoke briefly about a job running longer than the time in between when the job gets called, which can lead to the job running almost constantly. What are some other issues we see with Agent jobs?

Overlap

As your server gets busier, and more and more reports are run through jobs on a schedule, and suddenly you're importing and exporting data for extensible application behavior, jobs are going to start overlapping. It's very easy to throw jobs onto the same schedules, since that's one less step (creating a new schedule) that you need to take to get the job set up. However, having all of the jobs running at the same time is going to be a terrible performance hit on your server.

I have written a stored procedure that goes to MSDB (which is where job information is kept), pulls back the jobs that run on a daily basis (as opposed to weekly or one time only), and creates a text-based Gantt chart that shows when jobs run and for how long (using an average of the runtimes found in the job history). Each column represents a ten-minute time period, and if a job starts and ends within that time period, you'll see a | mark. If it continues beyond that period, you'll see something like | - - - | across the corresponding time frame columns.

If you have run the setup script, have the SQL Server Agent running, and have left your instance running more than a day, you should have a job history with four fake jobs I created for this example. We can tell by running the stored procedure under debug mode first. Please use the code in Listing 8-1.

Listing 8-1. Calling the Job Overlap stored procedure in debug mode

```
EXECUTE sp_jobOverlap @debug=1;
```

Let's look at the first recordset, like the one shown in Table 8-1. We want to see if there are any values in the duration column, indicating that the jobs set up on our server have run at least once. Since there is data in all of the duration columns, all of our jobs have run at least once. Times have been truncated for ease of reading.

Table 8-1. *Job Overlap stored procedure debug output, first result set*

jobid	jobName	SchedtimeDelay	startTime	endTime	duration
1	HourlyOne	01:00:00	06:00:00	22:00:00	00:19:20
2	syspolicy_purge_history	23:59:00	02:00:00	23:59:59	00:00:02
3	ShortOne	00:02:00	08:00:00	20:00:00	00:00:59
4	NightlyMaintenance	23:59:00	22:00:00	23:59:59	01:12:39
5	TooLong	00:30:00	04:00:00	22:00:00	00:27:39

As we continue to scroll down in the output, the last recordset shows the actual distribution of when the jobs run during the day. A lot of these jobs start a bit later in the day than SQL Server's default start-of-day time, as shown by the startTime column in Table 8-1. So you'll probably need to scroll right a bit before you see the job runs start to show up with | and – characters. Figure 8-1 shows the time frame between 7:40 a.m. and 10:00 a.m.

07:40	07:50	08:00	08:10	08:20	08:30	08:40	08:50	09:00	09:10	09:20	09:30	09:40	09:50	10:00
		I	I					I	I					I
		I	I	I	I	I	I	I	I	I	I	I	I	
-	I	I	-	I	I	-	I	I	-	I	I	-	I	

Figure 8-1. *Job Overlap stored procedure output*

The layout of the final result set, shown in Figure 8-1, makes it easy to identify ten-minute periods that have more than one job running. Sometimes you have a "perfect storm" of every job on the system running at the same time. It is important to find any overlap areas and try to distribute the jobs (especially longer-running jobs) so that they never run at the same time as other jobs. One way to do this would be to change schedules so that instead of every job starting on the hour, start one job on the hour, one job 10 minutes after the hour, a third job 30 minutes after the hour, and so on. Another method is to go back to your boss and up the chain to understand how important it is for those jobs that run every 2 minutes to really run every 2 minutes. Would every hour actually be enough? Or if the data is used for twice-a-day reports, could you just run the job 30 minutes before the daily reports are run?

You should recheck the job distribution periodically by rerunning the Job Overlap stored procedure. Jobs will start running longer over time, as data in the database builds up. This can cause overlap in areas where we didn't previously have issues. Awareness is the key to being able to be proactive, and to fix the problem before your boss is standing at your desk!

Summary

SQL Server Agent is a great tool for scheduling code to run at predetermined times. However, it is very important to understand both your environment and your jobs. Poorly planned timing of jobs, or jobs that exceed the actual business needs, can cause slowness in your entire environment and can sometimes be difficult to track down.

CHAPTER 9

External Influences

There will be places that call code or objects on the SQL Server that are not also on the SQL Server. Sometimes, companies use more than one SQL Server, but over time the need arises for the databases on different servers to "talk" to each other. Also, there may not always be a DBA, so the application developers write SQL code into the application instead of just calling an SQL object.

Linked Servers

Why do we use linked Servers? Sometimes, databases can be put on different servers because they generally have different workloads. The hardware could have been purchased or set up specifically for the workload of each set of databases. Maybe databases were initially developed by different departments, each of which had access to a specific SQL Server.

Whatever the case, inevitably someone will think it's a great idea to combine data from both servers/databases into a query, or perhaps many queries. There are some limitations which can require coding changes, unrelated to performance. Linked servers will not allow calls to user-defined table-valued or scalar functions. Depending on how heavily functions are used in your code, this could require significant rework effort.

Security

Generally, linked servers are set up to solve a problem quickly, and security isn't given a lot of thought. We think each server is secure in and of itself, so them sharing with each other is fine. However, this isn't the case. Local server logins should be set up in the linked server property page, and logins that are not specifically defined should not be allowed to connect. The setup can be complicated to do correctly while still allowing users to be able to perform the appropriate tasks.

© Lisa Bohm 2020
L. Bohm, *Refactoring Legacy T-SQL for Improved Performance*, https://doi.org/10.1007/978-1-4842-5581-0_9

Queries Joining Tables from Different Databases

When using a query across linked servers, the calling database will generally have filtering by using a WHERE clause on the query. However, sometimes SQL Server will just grab the entire table from the linked server, pull it back, and THEN apply the filtering in the WHERE clause. An execution plan of the query will clearly show when all of the rows are being returned from the linked server table. There are a few settings that should be examined to help minimize this issue, but those are beyond the scope of the book.

Earlier versions of SQL Server had issues with being able to read statistics across a linked server using a "reasonable" security model. Users had to have very high permissions in order to be able to get those statistics. This makes it very difficult for the optimizer to generate a good query plan when there's no information on how many records are being returned. Fortunately, Microsoft mitigated this with SQL Server 2012 SP1, so finding statistics with a lower permission level is less of a problem in more modern software versions.

Developers can use the OPENQUERY function to solve the filtering issue and make sure that filtering happens correctly on the remote server, before it sends back all of the rows. When using OPENQUERY, the statement actually runs on the linked server. When just calling the linked server tables directly, all of the code runs on the current server, not on the linked server, at least in SQL Server versions earlier than SQL Server 2017.

The behavior in newer versions seems to be based on how many rows will be returned, whether or not the filtering column is one of the columns joining the data between the two servers, and whether the filtering column is located on the remote server.

Network IO

Because as database professionals, we absolutely know that the cause of problems is always the network, right? Seriously though, the application is using the network to call SQL Server, which is using the network to pass data back. How many other applications are pushing data back and forth on the network? Any code on any machine that "speaks" to anything outside of that machine uses the network. Also, any IoT devices you might have also claim their piece of the network. We're just adding another possible point of performance issues or failure.

How Can We Fix This?

If both servers are VMs, it might be a good idea to decommission one of the VMs and make sure the databases that interact with each other are on the same instance of the same server. This is the best long-term solution, and if it is possible, I'd highly recommend going this route.

If moving the linked database(s) to the same server isn't an option, then we get back to refactoring the code. There will be a bit of research involved, looking at execution plans and time to find the most painful code first. The plans should really show where using OPENQUERY will be helpful; simply look for many, many rows being returned that aren't in the final output of the query.

Creating stored procedures on the linked server, and calling them from the local server, is another strategy that can be used to force code to run on the linked server instead of the local server. While the call to the stored procedure runs on the local server, all of the code in the stored procedure on the linked server runs then on the linked server. This strategy can be an effective way to break out pieces of the code to target which server is the optimal place for that code to be run.

SQL Code Calls in the Application

Have you ever heard the term "ORM"? It stands for object-relational mapping, and ORMs are tools that developers use to simplify specifically SQL code writing. They are popular because developers can write code faster – the tool generates the database code for you, and you don't have to write the "CRUD" (Create, Read, Update, Delete) SQL. They can generate parameterized queries, which is a good thing. However, we frequently see performance issues in the SQL code that these tools generate. If developers are aware of these well-publicized issues, most of them can be avoided.

So What's the Problem?

In order to fix SQL performance problems with code in the application, we need to have access to both the source code for the application and also the ability to create a new build of the application. If the initial development of the application code didn't take some of the currently well-known issues into consideration, the code could be causing quite a bit of pain on the SQL Server and affect other applications by taking up too many resources on the SQL Server.

ORM Filtering Data on the .NET Side

Developers need to write their .NET code so that filtering of returned datasets is performed on the SQL Server end, before it passes back data records. Otherwise, SQL Server will pass back all records, and they will get filtered on the .NET side. The unfiltered query retrieve and sending the retrieved data back to the application are a lot of work that neither the database nor the network should have to do. Devs also need to be aware of datatypes, because using incorrect types can lead to implicit conversion performance issues. Additionally, using conventions like UPPER(column) to do filtering can make index use impossible, again leading to performance issues.

ORM RBAR

When the application needs a parent object with associated child objects (think of a post and all of the associated responses), developers need to be aware of the chosen ORM's use of lazy loading. What this means is that the parent object is retrieved first and then the child objects are retrieved one at a time. There are plenty of strategies to avoid this issue when needed. There may be times when you won't want to retrieve all the child objects unless they require interaction, so the lazy loading is just fine. In other cases, though, developers can force eager loading in the code.

Also, inserting data via an ORM will cause a separate INSERT statement for each row that is added. Not only is this a lot of work for SQL Server but it can cause a lot of bloat in your transaction log.

Déjà Vu

Some ORMs can run into the same types of issues we see in database code. One of these is mismatching datatypes. If the datatype isn't defined with the correct value in the ORM, the code it generates could cause the same implicit conversion we discussed earlier in the book.

This is also true for returning too many columns. Like in your query (and NOT like using SELECT *), the developer writing the .NET code needs to specify exactly which columns need to be returned, so the whole record doesn't get pulled back each time.

It's very tempting to dump all of your criteria into a .NET call, but only a single query will get generated with a very complex WHERE statement. This will result in the Query Optimizer being unable to come up with a good plan, and suboptimal runtimes will show up. This can be avoided if developers are very specific when they make their calls, and think about what a WHERE clause would look like to deliver the data they're requesting.

Guess What? Use Stored Procedures!

All ORMs now can call stored procedures. Even after focusing on mitigating the issues mentioned earlier, really poor SQL code can still be generated. This is where the developer pulls the code out of the application and calls a stored procedure instead. It is then up to us to write that stored procedure to be optimized.

Dynamic SQL

ORMs can generate dynamic SQL under certain circumstances. The application can also be written to generate dynamic SQL. The biggest issue with this is that SQL Server can't then store an execution plan in the plan cache for the query; even changing a single white space in code will cause SQL Server to generate a new query plan. A new plan each run is expensive in terms of the work SQL Server has to do. Also, the dynamic SQL code generation can lead to some very complex and suboptimized queries, depending on the circumstances in which the code was built (many variables, many NULLs, and so forth).

Dynamic SQL is wonderful for queries that have many statements in the WHERE clause, but should be written very carefully and all of the different possible permutations should be generated and tested.

Summary

SQL calls from outside of the instance your database resides on can bring some performance issues. Linked servers can split up your database loads to separate servers, which is good. However, these linked servers have some inherent performance issues if your SQL isn't written correctly.

SQL code in the application, whether written by developers or generated by an ORM, is difficult to fix because we need a developer to manipulate the application code, or pull the direct SQL call out of the application and instead have the application code call a stored procedure that we can have access to. In the first case, we can direct the developer on how to write the SQL code. In the second case, we can write the code into a stored procedure which we can then tune using strategies we learned in earlier chapters of this book!

Thank you for coming on this journey with me to travel through the world of database objects and external influences and T-SQL code. I hope that you learned some new strategies for dealing with your legacy monster of an application. The ability to move from a reactive strategy to a proactive strategy is important to any of our sanity and is something we will all continue to strive for. Best of luck in your journey!

Index

A, B, C

Agent jobs, 221
  backups, 222
  corruption check, 222, 224
  differential backups, 222
  DR plan, 221
  environment, 223
  good jobs, 221
  index and statistics maintenance, 222
  overlap, 224–226
    output, 226
    result set, 225
    stored procedure, 224
  purge jobs, 222
  strategies, 221
  transaction log backups, 222
Aggregate functions, *see* Functions
andTheKitchenSink function, 204, 205,
    207, 209, 210

D, E

DATEADD() function, 202, 203
Database views, *see* Views
Data truncation, 32–38
Disaster Recovery (DR) plan, 221
Documentation
  coding patterns
    calculations, 38–40
    checklist of, 29

CTE evaluation code, 42
database table, 30, 31
IN and LIKE operators, 43
join types and syntax, 42
loops/cursors, 41
native SQL server
  function, 44–47
NOT IN and NOT LIKE, 43
sorting operations, 43
subqueries, 38, 39
temporary tables/variables, 40
TOP and DISTINCT, 43
user-defined SQL objects, 44
WHERE clause, 44–47
DailySummaryReportPerMonth
  calculations, 58
  data calls, 56, 57
  datatypes, 57
  functional requirements, 56
  join syntax, 58
  loops/cursors, 58
  sorting operations, 59
  source code, 48–55
  subqueries, 58
  temporary table/variables, 58
  WHERE clauses, 59
datatype
  data truncation, 32, 33
  implicit conversion, 34–38
  width, 37

233

L. Bohm, *Refactoring Legacy T-SQL for Improved Performance*, https://doi.org/10.1007/978-1-4842-5581-0

Printed in the United States
By Bookmasters